The culmination of various aspects of health hazards and the esoteric studies resulted in the publication of his book *The Boiled Frog Syndrome – Your Health and the Built Environment* in 2001. (Also published in Portuguese in Brazil). This led to a commission to write a peer-reviewed paper by Elsevier Science Limited entitled *Health Hazards and Electromagnetic Fields in hospital design and equipment*. In 2007, Watkins published his book *The Authentic Tarot: Discovering Your Inner Self*.

His autobiography, *Getting A Life*, published in 2014, includes accounts of his travels into the Amazon, the Arctic and his Atlantic Ocean sailings. He lived in France for eight years and returned to London in 2014 where he lives with his wife. He continues to be engaged in RIBA matters, student works, and the role and status of the architect.

Find out more at authentictarot.com and thomassaunders.net

I0079661

THOUGHTS ON ARCHITECTURE MYTHS AND MANAGEMENT

THOMAS SAUNDERS

SilverWood

Published in 2020 by SilverWood Books

SilverWood Books Ltd
14 Small Street, Bristol, BS1 1DE, United Kingdom
www.silverwoodbooks.co.uk

ISBN 978-1-78132-956-6 (paperback)
ISBN 978-1-78132-957-3 (ebook)

British Library Cataloguing in Publication Data
A CIP catalogue record for this book is
available from the British Library

Page design and typesetting by SilverWood Books

THOMAS SAUNDERS qualified in 1956 as a chartered architect – Associate Royal Institute of British Architects (ARIBA). In 1961 he set up practice at home as Thomas Saunders Architect. Two years later he moved to rooms over a shop in East London and engaged a secretary, two day-release students and a graduate working for his Part 3 exam at the local School of Architecture in Walthamstow. The principal invited him to fill the vacant post for teaching the two hours a week, Part 3 Professional Practice, which included Business Management in the new 1963 curriculum. He continued for the next four years. He was elected a Fellow of the RIBA in 1967.

The practice expanded and was renamed The Thomas Saunders Partnership (TTSP) when Saunders promoted four senior managers to full partnership. By 1982 it had developed into an international practice, with offices in London, Paris, Dubai and Kuwait. The 130 staff included the four partners managing the individual design teams, interior specialists, graphics designers, an office manager running the administration department and a separately managed PR/marketing unit. TTSP was one of the first practices to install CAD.

As the Senior Partner, Saunders realised he had promoted himself to a level of incompetence: he was no longer a hands-on practising architect. Robert Townsend's book *Up the Organization* advocated all chairmen and CEOs to leave after five years in the job, as the enthusiasm wanes, in order to allow others to rise up the business. Having read Joseph Campbell's quote, 'The real killer in life is when you find yourself at the top of the ladder and realise it is leaning against the wrong wall,' Saunders knew he had to explore new challenges.

In 1984 he resigned, severed all connections with the practice, and left it in the capable hands of the four remaining partners. (TTSP continues to be a thriving international practice in 2019.) He set up a company as an independent consultant acting as client representative and project director. He also served on the board of City Merchant Developers Limited.

He studied for an Advanced Certificate in environmental design and crime prevention and, in 2005, as a newly elected RIBA Client Design Advisor (CDA), a Russian developer appointed him to review a major housing development near Moscow's city centre. He is a professional remote viewer, field dowser and trainer. Thomas Saunders Consultants Limited was closed in 2017.

For much of his professional life, Saunders has explored the bonds linking architecture, the human experience, health, the authentic Tarot, the natural world and perennial teachings. His writings and seminars deliver presentations based on the design principles of Plato's seven liberal arts, of Vitruvius and the esoteric mystery school teachings. They aim to recover the perennial, covert, esoteric wisdom of the arts and sciences that have been taught throughout the ages.

Goethe's dictum, 'Architecture is frozen music', prompted him to research the fundamental principles of design, geometry and the structure of a building based on harmonic ratios, musical intervals and proportional volumes. These he found to resonate with the same harmonic ratios in human bodies to create a life-enhancing environment. His journey also led him to the profound symbolic language of the archetypes in the Tarot's authentic form and its teachings about the human psyche, human nature and life's journey from naivety to wisdom.

These thoughts are not the truth.
They may be a likely story.

CONTENTS

Forewords   12

Acknowledgements   14

Introduction   15

PART I
Thoughts on Architecture with Architects   23

1   The Cosmic Energy Fields   25

2   Perennial Mystery Schools   32

3   The Megalithic Ages   37

4   The Bronze and Iron Ages   40

5   The Golden Age of Greece   45

6   Empirical Rome   50

7   The Medieval Ages   57

8   The Renaissance   62

9   The Age of Enlightenment   69

10   The Age of Demarcation   73

11   The Age of Globalisation   80

PART II
Thoughts on the Professional Institutions 89

12	The Royal Institution of Chartered Surveyors	91
13	The Architects Registration Board	94
14	The Royal Institute of British Architects	101
15	The RIBA's New Code of Professional Conduct	109
16	The Clients	114

PART III
Thoughts on the Architect in Practice 119

17	The Role of the Architect	121
18	The Architect in Practice	128
19	Leadership and Management	136
20	Organisation Structures	147
21	Ethics	154

PART IV
Thoughts on Myths and Management 159

22	Myths, Folk Wisdom and Archetypes	161
23	The Allegorical Frescoes	165
24	Meet the Archetypes	169

PART V
Afterthoughts   179

25   Today's Challenges   181

26   Intuition and the Art of Knowing   189

Appendices   201

FOREWORDS

Thomas Saunders takes us on a fascinating journey through the myths and management of architecture.

We are immersed in architecture every day of our life. It surrounds us and affects us twenty-four hours a day, be it physically, psychologically or spiritually. It has been and should be the role of the architect to ensure we are living in spaces improve our lives and well-being. However, the importance, the role and the skill-set of the architect has diminished over time. This has provoked conversation for many architects in recent years. Thomas Saunders' review of the past shines a light on the evolving role of the architect. It brings a new and unique perspective to the mystics of architecture and the need for a successful and suitable leadership. Simultaneously, it hints: What is the future role of the architect?

Laura Bell, MA (Hons) March PGDip ARB RIBA

This book will resonate with most commercial architects in practice – particularly the newer generations.

Architects' greatly reduced incomes, following the 1983 Big Bang [deregulation of London's finance industry] and deregulation of the RIBA scale of fees, led to many practices abdicating their traditional responsibilities. Appropriately skilled staff were less often employed, and a degree of arrogance meant that our core duties were viewed as unattractive chores, without giving credence to the undoubted importance of the construction phase in the minds of our clients, which allowed project managers and quantity surveyors to take over. In turn, cash-saving clients have off-loaded design responsibilities and risks to contractors and others without appropriate skills. The result has also contributed to the dissipation of project leadership.

Saunders' book is a great summary of the malaise we've found ourselves in during most of my professional career. It certainly stimulates our thinking about what happens in the future.

Tim Jennings, Fellow Chartered Society of Designers,
Fellow RSA, retiring director TTSPPrice

ACKNOWLEDGEMENTS

My special thanks to my wife, Narin Gylman, and to Laura Bell, Tim Jennings and Professor Derek Clements-Croome for their helpful reading, encouragement and valuable comments. Grateful thanks to the many people, including Derek Salter, Past President and Hon Secretary, ACA, Dian Small, RIBA Director, the RIBA North London Architects Group, Peter Ullathorne and Allan Leiper, for their views and experiences of the professions and industry.

INTRODUCTION

'The principles of architecture are simply the principles of life.'
Frank Lloyd Wright

Our DNA shows traces of a continuing link with our ancestral Homo sapiens, who separated from prehistoric cave dwellers and became hunter-gatherers. In 1964, the Museum of Modern Art in New York commissioned Bernard Rudofsky, the Austrian–American writer, architect, teacher and social historian, to exhibit his extraordinary collection of photographs and drawings showing the evolution of building shelters, dwellings and urban developments since earliest times. The exhibition, *Architecture Without Architects*, was also published in book form by Doubleday & Company, New York. According to Rudofsky, we emerged from living in caves after witnessing our cousins, the anthropomorphous apes, building sheltered platforms (beavers did not get their idea of building a dam by watching human dam-builders at work). Human beings also have a primordial instinct to build shelters. We have always striven to create a social and physical environment that fulfils our physical, emotional, intellectual and spiritual needs. Rudofsky suggested that these early dwellings were produced by the spontaneous and continuing activity of communities with a common heritage, which accords with Plato's view that *eidos* (ideas) are pure mental forms imprinted in the soul before it is born into the world.

However, when so-called prehistory ended about 10,000 years ago, the mystics of the early urban civilisations developed advanced cosmological alignments, geometry and mathematics in the designs of their monuments and buildings. The Megalithic architects of, say, Stonehenge and the Bronze and Iron Ages, and the healer/priest architects who conceived the purpose, function and geometry of the *etheric* (sacred) body of the temples of Minerva, Angkor Wat and the Gothic cathedrals, were masters of geomancy. All were initiates of the ancient mystery schools. They respected Planet Earth as an intelligent living organism and saw that everything in the universe, including human beings, had a common, interconnecting bond. The patterns and movement of the heavenly bodies are a macrocosmic mirror reflection of life on Earth down to the microcosmic level of the sub-atomic world. In other words, the natural patterns, rhythms, proportions and geometry found in nature and the natural world are repeated throughout the universe. These architects would have had a profound understanding of the principles of health and well-being, and 'divine harmony' in the built environment, which are quintessential to the concept of any building, whether ecclesiastical or secular, and whatever the style or period. The perennial wisdom of esoteric teachings in every culture from antiquity and the early Dionysian and Eleusinian mystery schools of ancient Greece to the present day are based on fundamental physics, metaphysics and the nature of reality. Plato and Vitruvius were just two notable mystery school initiates.

From 400 BC, Plato's mysticism and philosophy of mind, soul, nature and universal order has shaped Western thought and influenced the major transitions of Christian theology, Islamic philosophy and the Renaissance. Six hundred years after Plato, the Roman architect and engineer, Vitruvius, published *The Ten Books of Architecture*. The book was a teaching manual and a partially covert treatise on the tenets of the arts and the fundamental principles of design. He set out a complete curriculum of the arts, sciences, matters of health, security, morality and spiritual development, as well as building construction and engineering, that was essential for an architect-engineer of the Roman Empire to study.

The book was 'lost' until the Florentine Poggio Bracciolini came across an edition in the St Gall Abbey library in Switzerland in 1414. Alberti referred to it in 1450 and an edition was published in Latin in Rome in 1486. Daniele Barbaro translated the work in 1556. It became the bible for the multidisciplined Renaissance polymaths. None had been formally taught to be professional architects, but they had a deep sense and understanding of the subtle interplay and common bond of energies by which the cosmos functions as a harmonious whole. They also knew how to manifest the natural vibrations in the buildings they designed to create a harmonic resonance with human beings and the natural world, to sustain healthy living conditions that would feed our spirit.

The natural world turns in cycles, continually ebbing and flowing from chaos to order and back to chaos. The defining spirit of the eighteenth and early nineteenth centuries was the materialism of the Age of Enlightenment and the Industrial Revolution, which changed the mainstream beliefs and promoted attitudes that human beings and all living organisms, including our planet, consisted of a body with no soul or spirit to the point where the soul was not appropriate for rational study. (Even now, orthodox human psychology recognises neither the soul nor higher consciousness.) The concept and mind-set of the Earth as a living, intelligent energy was transformed to that of treating it as a lifeless, mechanistic mass. These cultural changes first challenged and then discarded the perennial teachings of the fundamental principles of design as anachronistic. Perennial wisdom continues to be ignored, as having little or no relevance to the twenty-first century.

Newtonian science and physics became compartmentalised when philosophy, metaphysics, mathematics and geometry began to be taught as specialised, separate sciences. When we entered the new world of specialisation, it led to the establishment of allied professional institutions, including the Royal Institute of British Architects (RIBA) as a chartered body in 1837. Schools of architecture were set up for the seven years of training and education required to become a professional architect as:

> one who strategically conceived as well as tactically controlled the total design of the setting, the exterior, the interior design, decoration and furnishing and their related costs and buildability that will satisfy its function, purpose and needs.

Does this describe the teaching or the work, practice and services of the majority of today's professional architects? Do Western schools of architecture teach humanistic philosophy, the fundamental principles of design and the essence of leadership? Has fragmentation and the erosion of the traditional role of the master architect left many projects to chance in terms of whether a building will be spiritually uplifting and conducive to health and well-being or whether it will be disturbing, inherently sick and detrimental to all those in occupation?

As early as 1964, Bernard Rudofsky understood the trend:

> Part of our troubles [since the nineteenth and twentieth centuries] results from the tendency to ascribe to architects – or, for that matter, to all specialists – exceptional insight into problems of living when, in truth, most of them are concerned with problems of business and prestige. Besides, the art of living is neither taught nor encouraged […] Above all, it is the *humaneness* of this architecture [vernacular, communal art and common heritage] that ought to bring forth some response in us.
>
> *Architecture Without Architects*, Preface

Since the mid-twentieth century, the culture, style of business practice and globalisation has dramatically changed the role of the architect. With the notable exceptions of the well-established and globally celebrated firms of 'starchitects', the role of the majority of practices in the UK and the USA, has become marginalised, undervalued, underpaid and generally held in low regard. What has contributed to their decline?

These questions are the major concerns of today's British and American architects and their institutions. Setting aside the inevitable variations in the quality of service and expertise offered by architects, the compartmentalisation and expansion of specialisation required of a development's project team have also contributed to the marginalisation, loss of status and the decline in earnings for today's twenty-first century architects. It could also be said that fortuitously the support of the many technically well-equipped project team specialists allows the architect more time and energy to expend on ingenuity and the essential elements of design and the fundamental principles to create healthy environments that nourish and uplift our spirits. Regrettably, it tends to become a burden when the architect is not the leader.

According to Phil Bernstein, the Associate Dean at Yale School of Architecture, the marginalisation and downgrading of architects, and the poor profit margins, are as prevalent in the USA as in Britain. The seven-year training of architects, doctors and lawyers is comparable but six to ten years after graduation lawyers and doctors will earn twice the salary of an architect.

By the 1930s, a qualified, chartered architect – an Associate of the RIBA – enjoyed the high esteem and social status of a professional person. (In the industry, the acronym ARIBA also meant, 'All Right I'm the Bloody Architect'). After six years, the principal or senior partner of an established practice could be eligible to be elected as a Fellow of the RIBA. The bond between the client and architect was recognised as being sacrosanct. When the site and design project meetings were chaired by a senior architect, it was not unusual for those around the table to rise when he or she entered the meeting room.

The RIBA imposed a scale of minimum fees for specific works, which was based on the value architects offered rather than market forces. Any architect reported to be undercutting the scale was offering unfair competition and would be hauled before the Ethics Committee. They could suffer severe penalties. Over the past four decades, the dismantling of the RIBA's traditional fee structure and colluding with the insidious takeover of the architect's strategic leadership role has contributed to the profession being marginalised and undervalued. Had architects been paid fees commensurate with their services and their expertise valued, would these roles have been offloaded or taken over by others? If so, it is no wonder the profession has become fragmented and, in certain sectors, has become virtually irrelevant. Undoubtedly, media coverage of collapsed buildings, local authority high-rise ghettoes and the Grenfell Tower fire have, over the years, unfairly contributed to architects' poor social standing. The TV programme *Grand Designs* is all about the buildings' owners; the architect's role in producing the projects' design and documentations is hardly, if ever, mentioned or acknowledged.

In her 2018 book, *Why Architects Matter*, Professor Flora Samuel (the first Vice-President for Research at the RIBA) says it is essential to ensure clients, project managers and the general public understand and appreciate the distinguishing and distinguished values of architects and architecture. The metaphysical values architects need to offer are the professional services that create ecologically and environmentally sound, sustainable, life-enhancing buildings and to do so, the training and education of architects must also embrace these values. Equally important is the need for the Architects Registration Board (ARB) and the RIBA to continue their ongoing review of the curriculum and syllabus for the teaching and training of architects.

The profession's challenge and opportunity are to synthesise and bring together the wonders of modern technology with the integrity of perennial wisdom, the understanding of human beings and the eternal laws of nature and the universe. Significantly, the RIBA's recently updated code of conduct responds to Western society's re-awakening to a way of life that is reacting to pure materialism, globalisation and climate change. It is, or should be, a positive opportunity for the architect to once again become the master builder.

Works cited

Bernard Rudofsky. *Architecture Without Architects*, Doubleday, 1964.

Flora Samuel. *Why Architects Matter*, Routledge, 2018.

PART I

THOUGHTS ON
ARCHITECTURE WITH ARCHITECTS

CHAPTER 1
THE COSMIC ENERGY FIELDS

Architecture: the wisdom of nature and the science of well-being
Our planet is a giant magnet surrounded by the ever-changing magnetic fields of other planets, the magnetosphere of solar wind particles and the Earth's molten core of magma. The interaction of these fields creates the extremely low frequencies (ELFs) that have a strong influence on single-celled organisms, plant life, animals and human beings. Electro-magnetic fields affect all biological and physical processes, health, behaviour patterns and the ability to orientate a position in space. At a fundamental level, everything living on our planet, as well as rocks and metals, emits its own life-sustaining, weak electromagnetic field.

Every human cell operates like a battery, sending out signals to activate the constant interchange of biochemical and bioelectrical processes. Human blood contains ions that have a range resonance with the Earth's geomagnetic field and an alternating field ranging between 1Hz and 500Hz. If an electrical or magnetic field is applied near this resonance frequency it can impact upon the lymphocyte cells, which, in turn, affects the immune system response and may be a factor in cases of lymphatic leukaemia and other diseases.

It is evident that prehistoric peoples and other traditional cultures were acutely aware of the Earth's energy fields. Their sites established for sacred ceremonies and human habitation were locations where the positive energy fields could be used for healing, fertility, food production and good health. They were also aware of those non-benign areas to be avoided where negative energies were present. The tribal societies that still exist today in remote regions, or even in some Third World countries, are also well aware of these natural forces and respectfully co-exist with them.

Low-frequency waves of electromagnetic telluric currents cover the whole planet. One such energy, known as the Schumann Wave is thought to be the interaction between Earth and the ionosphere, creating a magnetic radiation resonating at the same or similar frequencies to human brainwaves. Astrophysicist Dr Percy Seymour proposed a model that showed how the reaction of the planets to the magnetic fields of the Moon, Sun and Earth impinges on the pineal gland's super sensitivity to weak magnetic field changes that influence our state of mind, moods and emotions. The pineal gland is ultra-sensitive to light and extremely faint electromagnetic fields. This master gland controls all the other endocrine glands, secreting the flow of hormones through the body via the autonomic nervous system, which operates the release of the cocktail of chemicals that affect our metabolism, emotions and moods of elation or depression.

Light is a primary source of energy and a form of electro-magnetic radiation. One of the great mysteries of biology is how the cells in our body communicate by low-level light transmission. In her *Living the New Science* podcast, Lynne McTaggart cites research by the late German physicist Fritz-Albert Popp:

> All living things, from single-celled plants to human beings emit a tiny current of photons, tiny particles of light. He labelled them biophoton emissions and believed he had uncovered the primary communication channel of living organisms. This faint radiation, rather than biochemistry, is the true driving force in orchestrating and coordinating all cellular processes in the body. This suggests that living consciousness might have a major effect on the ultra-sensitive microprocessor technology.

Life on Earth is a constituent part of an integrated universal radiation system in which terrestrial energy fields interact with fields of cosmic energy – alpha, beta, gamma and neutron rays with light, infrared, microwave radiation – originating from the Sun, Moon, planets and the Milky Way. All these forms of radiation create 'zones of resonance', or 'patterns of interference', which affect all physical matter, including rocks, soil, plants, animals and human beings. Without these interacting, unseen and extremely weak fields of subtle energy we would not exist, plants could not survive, birds and animals could not navigate, turtles could not return after thirty years at sea to the beach where they were hatched, and the tides of the oceans would not rise and fall.

Geological structures and variations to the natural landscape also interact and create modifications to the Earth's energy field. Therefore, at certain times and in certain places the vibrations or field strengths will be irregular. The uniqueness of every location is determined by trees, mountains, hills, rivers, underground streams, rock formations, stones and other changes in the environment such as buildings.

The magnetosphere does not rotate with the Earth. As the same side is always facing the Sun, the geomagnetic field at the Earth's surface constantly changes during the course of a twenty-four-hour period. The Earth's position relative to the Sun, the phases of the Moon, the movement of other planets, solar flares and magnetic storms also create variations in the Earth's magnetic field. The path of the solar wind deflected by the Earth streams out into space like the tail of a comet, setting up variations in the cosmic force fields that, again, change the strength of the magnetic field as it rotates, thus affecting at a subtle level the biological systems of all living things.

Experiments with plants and animals have shown the effects of weak radiation emanating from cosmic and terrestrial sources, indicating that various organisms, mammals and other marine life are indeed influenced by pervasive weak geomagnetic fields. (Plants seem able to sense the small geomagnetic changes originating in the ionosphere when the Sun rises at dawn.) Not all living organisms have an adverse reaction to negative energy fields, but human beings and many other species need a positive and coherent energy input to maintain health and vitality. A negative signal can set up an interference pattern causing a malfunction of the extremely weak electromagnetic field effects on the brainwaves and cells of the body.

Fault lines occur where the pressure on the strata of the Earth's surface is relieved, causing piezoelectrical discharges to be squeezed out from the rocks, ionising the air to create luminous rays, 'eerie lights' and fireballs. Eyewitness accounts of these ghostly nocturnal lights include 'will-o-the-wisp' and 'curious flames'. Modern UFO sceptics are convinced that these many sightings have been located where natural fault lines occur: the blazing lights associated with the phenomenon are actually Earth lights or flashes of energy erupting from geological piezoelectrical activity.

A feeling of being icy cold in a 'haunted' room, despite the thermometer recording normal temperatures, may be due to a rogue electromagnetic field reacting on the hypothalamus – the gland regulating our body temperature controlled by the pineal gland. A weak electromagnetic energy field can also enhance psychic processes and induce altered states of consciousness due to the interaction with the pineal and pituitary gland secretions. The pituitary gland governs the onset of puberty when hormonal changes affect the degree of calcification in the body and our teeth and bones begin to harden. Hair, bone, feathers and horn – often used in occult shamanic practices – produce faint electromagnetic pulses that interact with external electromagnetic fields. When we are frightened our hair stands on end! Even the most minute and extremely weak shifts in the natural geomantic field strength, or an artificially generated electrical field, can interfere with the brain's wave patterns, triggering the release of endocrine gland secretions that affect us biologically and emotionally.

Why do some locations have a magical 'aura' that puts us in touch with a natural vitality or a sense of harmony and well-being, whereas certain other places can make us feel perturbed, uncomfortable, or even ill? Sites associated with magical, psychic activities and other phenomena, such as haunted houses, also seem to occur in locations along geological fault lines.

Although the local geology may be somewhat different now, it is clear that through the ages, from the Megalithic peoples to the present day, settlements were sited at locations where positive energy fields existed. Ancient shamans, priests and 'magicians' were relied on to dowse for beneficial sites and to neutralise a location or cleanse a site of the 'bad vibes' that were perhaps due to natural elements or where a violent battle or accident had taken place. This highly developed intuitive knowledge of and sensitivity to energy fields evolved into a spiritual reverence and 'sacred earth' culture that persisted well into Medieval Europe.

North American Indian culture, like most other Earth traditions, is based on a mystical philosophy of the soul's integration and at-oneness with the cosmic forces and nature. Forests, rivers, rocks, mountains and sky personify invisible creatures; the Sun symbolises the spirit of goodness and its associated concepts. Their initiation rites are not dissimilar to the mystery school initiations of ancient Egypt. Through the rites of passage a neophyte can begin to comprehend the symbolism that is everywhere for those who have eyes to see and ears to hear. The Upanishads, one of the ancient Hindu sacred texts, say, 'It is impossible for us to learn elsewhere what we are incapable of learning within our bodies.' In other words, our body is a microcosmic model of the whole universe.

Works cited

Lynne McTaggart. *Living the New Science* podcast, Show Notes, Episode 3. http://lynnemctaggart.podbean.com

Sir Percy Seymour. *The Paranormal: Beyond Sensory Science*, Penguin, London, 1992.

Suggested further reading

A. Dubrov. *The Geomagnetic Field and Life,* Plenum Press, New York, 1998.

J. Thurnell-Read. *Geopathic Stress*, Element Books, Dorset, 1996.

Guy Underwood. *The Pattern of the Past*, Museum Press, London, 1968.

Paul Broadhurst, Gabriele Trso. *Axis of Heaven*, Mythos, Cornwall, 2016.

Mircea Eliade. *Shamanism: Archaic Techniques of Ecstasy.* Princeton University Press, 1974.

Thomas Saunders. Chapter 3 in *The Boiled Frog Syndrome*, Wiley-Academy, 2002.

CHAPTER 2

PERENNIAL MYSTERY SCHOOLS

The word 'mystery' is derived from the Greek *muo*, meaning 'to close the lips or eyes'. The ancient word 'mystes' is the probable root of the modern word 'mystic', meaning a seeker of truth, and to the Greeks 'truth' meant the whole cosmic system. The perennial mystery school teachings were a codified system of wisdom that integrated the arts, sciences and spirituality as a common bond with nature and the universe.

The lineage of today's professional architects can be traced back to the esoteric teachings of the ancient mystery schools, from the gentlemen architects of the eighteenth century; to the polymaths of the Renaissance; to the healer-priests of the Middle Ages; to the geomantic masters of the Iron and Bronze Ages and beyond to the Neolithic and Mesolithic periods of the Stone Ages. Throughout history, mystics have endeavoured to make sense of the great truths of nature, the principles of natural lore and the forces of the universe on which depended the health and well-being of their cultural group or tribe. To simplify the fundamental principles, the mystics personified the teachings as archetypal gods and goddesses. Generations of shamans, healer-priests, geomancers and master builders – the forebears of the professional architect – taught and practised the accumulated wisdom found in our own rich Western European heritage of geomancy, metaphysics, mystical teachings and literature. Tribal elders – the shaman and the healer-priest mystics – are the guardians and teachers of the mysteries of life who have always been with us. Even contemporary Western elders or initiators into the sacred arts can still be found, although they maintain a low profile.

Prehistoric stone circles of Britain, the Sphinx and the pyramids of Giza, the Mesoamerican pyramids, the temples of Angkor Wat, and the major cathedrals in France are not only linked by common dimensions related to the geometry and distances of the Earth to the planets, they also reflect the patterns of certain constellations in the sky. The architects were initiates of the mystery schools associated with Dionysus, Isis, Sabazius, Cybele and Eleusis. The School of Dionysus, established in 1,000 BC, spread across Asia Minor, Egypt, India, the Roman Empire, Central Europe and England. Initiates included Pythagoras, Plato, Vitruvius, other great philosophers and the travelling master masons of the Middle Ages. The perennial teachings continued the tradition of designing buildings according to the fundamental principles of the sacred arts and sciences to create architecture that symbolised a spiritual, mystical concept expressing a human relationship with nature, the cosmos and the divine world – an attempt, if you will, to create a heaven on Earth. These fundamental principles of design are commonly found in every period or style of architecture.

A mystery school provided the map and compass bearings for those about to explore both the natural phenomena of the outer world and their own inner world of human nature and the psyche. The teachings recognised three principle levels of reality: the *exoteric*, physical realm of matter; the *mesoteric* realm of the mind and spirit; and the *esoteric* realm of mysticism. In essence, mystery school teachings were a progressive initiation from the profane to the sacred realms, while the curricula of the great academics of the Hermetic, Pythagorean Western tradition and those of India and China of the Eastern civilisations were fundamentally the same as the shamanic tribal societies of, say, the Australian outback or jungles of South America. Their purpose was to guide the neophyte along the heroic path of spiritual rites of initiation into the mysteries of our relationship with nature, the cosmos and a divine spirit, and to reawaken our soul through remembrance.

Every culture has had its own form of mystery school teachings where both the young and adults are initiated into the secrets and ancient wisdom of the tribe or society. In every community and civilisation the mystics and sages were, and still are, deeply versed in the laws of nature and the universe. Without having a fundamental understanding of these laws, we cannot live intelligently. The masters and custodians of the schools passed down universally sacred knowledge as it evolved from generation to generation and taught secret practices to those who had reached appropriate levels of ordered discipline. The teachings were profound, potent and powerful, and remained almost entirely oral in order to protect the knowledge from being misunderstood or unscrupulously misused by the uninitiated. The purpose was not to conceal the truth of nature's secrets, nor to mystify, but for the initiate to fully understand human beings as a microcosmic symbol of the whole universe. Such written material that was produced was couched in covert, symbolic language that would only be significant and comprehensible to initiates. From the most ancient peoples to the present day, secret schools of initiation into esoteric wisdom have flourished. Perennial wisdom is eternal: the mystical concept of a unified, interconnected, harmonious cosmos embracing the whole of existence persisted as an enduring wisdom. It continued through to the Renaissance up to the eighteenth century and, as ever, even today the seeds are always with us; like the seasons, sometimes they blossom, at other times they lie covert.

The arts and sciences of master building, mathematics, geometry, medicine, law, music and philosophy and astrology/astronomy can be traced back to the mystery school-initiated philosophers and priests who, according to the Egyptian theologian Origen, 'have a sublime and secret knowledge respecting the secret of God'. The ancient mystics went to extraordinary lengths to ensure that sacred knowledge was preserved for future generations and would be protected from uninitiated superstition and vandalism. Mathematics, geometry, astrology, harmonic ratios and hieroglyphics were symbols used by the masters of mystery schools to teach sacred knowledge. These teachings were concealed within the orientation, dimensions and symbolism of volume, spaces and decoration of buildings to encode the esoteric meanings of life, death and the universal laws.

Since the Age of Enlightenment, about three hundred years ago, the subjects of cosmology*, metaphysics and philosophy have become specialist subjects, no longer taught in the general syllabus of European universities. Today these integral aspects of design form no part of the curriculum in our schools of architecture; they are not even mentioned. Consequently, many practising architects have little or no understanding, or practical use for, the fundamental principles that created extraordinary architecture such as Stonehenge, the Great Pyramid of Giza, cathedrals, mosques and temples, as well as the great secular buildings still standing.

Suggested further reading

T. Taylor. *The Eleusinian and Bacchic Mysteries,* Wizards Bookshelf, San Diego, 1980.

Manly P. Hall. *The Secret Teachings of All Ages*, Philosophical Research Society, 1994.

Peter Wohlleben. *The Hidden Life of Trees*, HarperCollins, 2015.

* Astrology is the study of the movement and positions of the Sun, Moon, planets and stars; astronomy is the science of the celestial objects, space and astrophysics. Before the Enlightenment, they were synonymous. Astrology has been taught in universities for millennia and images of the zodiac date back to earliest times. The word 'cosmology' avoids ambiguity and argument.

CHAPTER 3
THE MEGALITHIC AGES

Megalithic architects

Britain has 286 Megalithic stone circles; of these, 235 are located within a mile of a geological fault or Earth fissure. Other structures acted as boundary markings, calendars and, perhaps, as instruments for influencing the weather, as well as being a focal point for religious practices. Before the Roman conquest of Britain and France, the ancient Celtic priesthood known as Druidism had been well established since early Megalithic times. Druids' esoteric knowledge embraced a deep understanding of cosmology, natural theology, geometry and the physical sciences. Their architect-master builder-priests were also physicians who used magnetism and herbal medicines as well as crude surgical instruments. They also worshipped the Sun and nature spirits and believed in the immortality of the soul. Julius Caesar was very hostile to their practices and eventually the Romans persecuted them out of mainland Europe and Britain. Those who escaped to Ireland survived only until the Christian missionaries arrived, but we can see that vestiges of the thousands of years of Druid Brotherhood and traditions are still with us today when they gather at Stonehenge for the equinoxes and solstices. Otherwise, Druidism remains a covert society.

Professor Keith Critchlow's *Time Stands Still* shows photographs of Neolithic granite stones carved to form a series of the regular mathematical symmetries known as the twelve Platonic solids (such as the tetrahedron, the icosahedron and dodecahedron). These stones were believed to have been used to teach three-dimensional mathematics, which predates Pythagoras and Plato by about a thousand years or so. They were on display in Edinburgh and are similar to stones in the Egyptian galleries of the British Museum. Professor Critchlow's more recent book, *The Knap of Howar and the Origin of Geometry*, written with Nicholas Cope, illustrates a Neolithic settlement excavated on the west coast of Papa Westray on one of the remote islands of Orkney in Scotland. The dwelling predates 3,500 BC. The architectural design shows evidence of a sophisticated knowledge of geometry, including the golden section.

In 1967, Alexander Thom, a Scottish professor of engineering, published the results of his meticulous surveys of many Megalithic stone circles in Britain, including Stonehenge. He discovered that the stones had been set with great precision and the ground plans were based on accurate geometrics and elaborations of the circle, ellipse and Pythagorean triangles to produce highly complex astrological alignments, later confirmed by astrophysicist Professor Fred Hoyle.

Works cited

Keith Critchlow. *Time Stands Still: New Light on Megalithic Science*, St. Martin's Press, New York, 1982.

Keith Critchlow, Nicholas Pope. *The Knap of Howar and the Origins of Geometry,* Kairos Publications, 2015.

Alexander Thom. *Megalithic Sites in Britain*, Clarendon Press, Oxford, 1970.

Suggested further reading

Don Robins. *Circles of Silence*, Souvenir Press, London, 1985.

Robin Heath. *Alexander Thom: Cracking the Stone Age Code*, Bluestone Press, 2003.

Thomas Saunders. *The Boiled Frog Syndrome*, Wiley-Academy, 2002, pp. 142-163.

CHAPTER 4
THE BRONZE AND IRON AGES

Bronze and Iron Age architects

It is misleading to refer to geomancy as the fortune-telling practices of Earth divination. The Bronze and Iron Age architects, known as masters of geomancy, were indeed acutely aware of the Earth's energy fields and understood the Earth's magnetic fields, global grid patterns and geopathic stress zones. The subterranean strata, water streams, natural features of the landscape, flora and fauna, prevailing winds and orientation were investigated and identified to ensure that the location and design of a building, whether it be a humble dwelling, majestic palace or temple of worship, would create the most harmonious influences for the health, well-being and prosperity of the occupants.

Ancient Hindu studies of life force, known as *prana*, carried by channels of energy called *nadis*, and India's long history steeped in the science of physics, chemistry, astronomy, astrology and symbolism, were the foundation of Vastu Shastra, the science of house-building: (*vastu* = house, *shastra* = science or technology). Comparable Eastern systems are known as *Feng Shui* in China; *Dai Ly* in Vietnam; and *Yattana* in Burma. In China, the high priests of Feng Shui were called

Dragon Masters and were highly trained initiates of the art and science of esoteric teachings. In European culture the geomancers were *locator civitatis*; the Celts knew them as wizards or shamans. While the ancient Celtic tradition and Vastu Shastra are thought to predate Feng Shui, all are based on the same perennial tenets that encompassed agriculture, architecture, interior design, landscape and medicine. Feng Shui is still taught and practised in East Asian schools of architecture.

Sanskrit – 'the language of the gods' – is the sacred language of the Hindu religion founded about 5,000 years ago. It has highly differentiated terminology to describe extraordinary states of consciousness, mental and spiritual processes and subtle body physiology for which there are no known equivalents in the languages of the West. *Chakra* (meaning wheel or circle) is the Sanskrit word for the power centres located in the physical body. There is a strong correspondence between the endocrine glands and the Hindu *chakra* system. Just as the quality of *prana* flowing through the chakras determines a person's health, the free flow of the breath of life through landscapes and interiors is affected by the location, orientation, siting and layout of a building. A damaging effect may be caused by disturbing the natural tellegro-geognostic energy lines in the terrain, as this too can influence *prana*'s direction and flow. The life force, known as *Ond*, may be of Celtic/Saxon origin. The Japanese call it *Ki* and in Chinese it is *Ch'i* or *Qi*). The sum total of Earth energies, cosmic radiation, the heavenly bodies, air, water, human emotions and activity, and the whole of the natural world is a life force carried on the wind (*Feng*) and contained by water (*Shui*) known as 'dragon lines'. A Dragon Master identified these subtle forces and deflected, dispersed and neutralised the negative *Sha Ch'i* to allow the positive *Shen* force to flow. A fourteenth-century text devoted to dowsing mentions the various diseases associated with geopathic stress. The little-known Celtic geomantic tradition has been researched and well documented by Nigel Pennick in *Earth Harmony: Places of Power, Holiness and Healing.*

The Dragon Master architects had a deep insight and awareness of the uniqueness of the nature, spirit and soul of a given location or building by dowsing, feeling, seeing, listening, smelling and tasting everything about the subtle energies of the place and its environment, whether the building was a house, office, hospital, school, bridge, tunnel or a new town. The vibrant energy centre or nucleus (known in Western tradition as the *anima loci,* or the soul of a place) is identified as the heart or spiritual focal point of the property.

Geomantic laws can be thought of as a highly sophisticated set of building codes, similar to our modern-day building by-laws and public health regulations, except that they go far beyond the merely practical, physical aspects of creating a healthy building. The codes also address the whole range of subtle energy fields that affect us physically, mentally and spiritually. The codes set out a building's or new town's most auspicious and beneficial location and directions for the best orientation for ventilation, the thickness of walls, the safest soil for foundations, the healthiest layout of the dwelling and the methods to prevent ill health from the bitter cold winds from the North. At least ninety per cent of the codes would be supported by modern science. They also included the proportions and shapes of the interior rooms, the colours, lighting, textures, the flow of air, that have a sum total impact on the mind, body and spirit of all those who enter the building.

So, is all this mumbo-jumbo, superstitious divination, or did these architects have a profound understanding of the characteristics and moods of nature that developed a codified set of rules and guidelines to create environmental conditions in tune with cosmic forces? (Quantum theory says that everything in the universe – from living organisms to solid rocks – is a varying, condensed form of sunlight.) Physiologically, biologically and psychologically we are profoundly affected by the quality and quantity of light and colour determined by a building's location, orientation and interior spaces. The light penetrating our eyes through to the endocrine glands regulates our life processes: the pineal, pituitary, thyroid, hypothalamus and adrenals. These glands and receptors disseminate our physical, mental and psychic processes including our behavioural responses and perceptions of the myriad of stimuli at every moment of the day. We can 'hear' the beat and rhythm of inaudible sounds, so we can 'see' the invisible geometric constructs of an object or building.

The flow of fresh air through a building will increase the negative ions that induce a sense of vitality (Appendix 1); an aquarium, fountain or bowl of flowers will maintain a healthy humidity level, reduce static electricity and inspire a feeling of movement and life. Morning sunlight streaming through a window, the enjoyment of beneficial energy flows and a clean, uncluttered environment, free from dust-collecting papers and other paraphernalia, avoids vermin and bugs; the conscious placement of a few chosen objects in a room can be a constant reminder of the orderliness of the natural world about us. When we become aware of our interaction with nature and the rhythms of life, it heightens our vitality and is conducive to a positive, uncluttered state of mind, which, at a subtle level, affects our thought processes and feelings of optimism. Undoubtedly, a clean, orderly house, properly arranged and orientated to give good natural light and air with harmonious colours will create a stress-reduced environment in the same manner that plants thrive or fail depending upon the quality of the soil and the climatic conditions – wind, water, sunlight and the changing seasons.

Works cited

Nigel Pennick. *The Ancient Science of Geomancy*, Thames & Hudson, 1979.

N.H. Sahasrabudhe, R.D. Mahatme. *Secrets of Vastushastra*, Sterling Publishers Pvt Ltd India, 1998.

Lillian Too. *The Complete Illustrated Guide to Feng Shui*, Element Books, 1997.

Nigel Pennick. *Earth Harmony: Places of Power, Holiness and Healing*, Capall Bann Publishers, 1997.

Suggested further reading

Tom Graves. *Dowsing and Archaeology*, Turnstone Books, 1980.

Gustav Freiherr Von Pohl. *Earth Currents: Causative Factor of Cancer and Other Diseases*, Frech-Verlag Stuttgart, 1932.

CHAPTER 5

THE GOLDEN AGE OF GREECE

The philosopher architects

In Greek philosophy *arche* is the primary element and first principle that encompasses the attributes and value of all things: it is the source of action. The Parthenon, a temple dedicated to the goddess Athena in the fifth century BC, was built over the ruin of an older temple destroyed by Persian invaders. The siting of the Parthenon is aligned to the Hyades cluster of stars in the constellation of Taurus. The building, with its extraordinary optical refinements and links to the golden section and the great Egyptian pyramid, is one of the world's greatest cultural monuments, and yet the architects, Ictinus and Callicrates – thought to have been initiates of the Eleusinian Mystery School – are rarely noted or mentioned; whereas their client, Pericles, the statesman and general, is well known. (Nothing new there then.) Ictinus, Callicrates and many other Greek architects were immersed in the golden age of philosophy and particularly the work of Pythagoras's geometry and Plato's principles of the seven liberal arts, revealed in his book *Timaeus*. Plato also published the geometry of the golden section and again was severely criticised for breaking the strictly covert oral tradition. His academy in Athens survived from 385 BC until its dissolution by Justinian in 529 AD.

The Seven Liberal Arts

The seven liberal arts were divided into the trivium (three) and the quadrivium (four), the two numbers representing the trinity of heaven with the four-foldedness or cube of Earth. The art and science of the trivium are grammar, rhetoric and logic (or dialectic): all three relate to the proper use of language.

Grammar   The exact choice of words or construction of phrase to unambiguously convey a precise meaning as an expression, in noble language, of the innermost thoughts, ideals and ideas that personify goodness.

Rhetoric   The quality of communicating in beautiful and convincing language, style, analysis and presentation an expression of beauty.

Logic   The organisation of language in search of the truth by means of the power of deduction and reasoned debate without the egotistical desire to win an argument; it makes full use of intellectual facilities to discover truth.

The arts and science of the quadrivium are arithmetic, geometry, harmonics or music, and cosmology. All four transcend language, express universal truths (in any language there can be no argument that $2 + 2 = 4$), and are fundamental to understanding the nature of existence.

Arithmetic   Pure number, known as the Queen of the Sciences. Arithmetic is the key to magnitude, proportion and the mystery of the universal order.

Geometry   Number in form or space, and the harmony and rhythm of angles and the philosophy of organisation. Geometry means 'measure of the Earth'.

Music   Number in time governed by the laws of harmonics, mathematical ratios and musical progressions expressed in the elliptical orbits, rhythms and movement of the celestial bodies. Reputedly, Pythagoras invented the monochord to explain the musical harmonic spacing of the cosmos. His concept of music of the spheres was developed in the seventeenth century by Johannes Kepler in his *Harmonices Mundi* in which he describes his Third Law of Planetary Motion. (In other words, discordance and cacophony reflect our conflicts with nature and the environment.)

Cosmology   Number in time and space, which expresses the interrelationship between the microcosm of human beings, and the macrocosm of the universe. While Plato's cosmology was based

47

on the geocentric views of Ptolemy and Arab astronomy, this changed with Copernicus, Kepler and Galileo; but the philosophical concept remained constant and reflected the awesomeness of unknown power.

The quadrivium – arithmetic, geometry, music and cosmology – was preparatory to the philosophy and wisdom of art and science. All four disciplines were regarded as an intrinsic entity, which would not be taught separately any more than the body would be regarded as separate from the soul and spirit. The soul formed a bridge between the physical and metaphysical worlds and mathematics was the interface between the invisible and the visible worlds.

IBM scientist Benoît Mandelbrot's book *The Fractal Geometry of Nature* illustrates the extraordinary mystical patterns of star constellations, islands, mountains and snowflakes, and shows how the growth of organisms on the macroscopic to the microscopic scale appears to be governed by repeating elementary laws of geometry. In his *Timaeus*, Plato had already discovered that these natural growth patterns corresponded to the orbits of heavenly bodies.

Works cited

Plato. *Timaeus and Critias*, Penguin Books, London, 1971.

Jamie James. *Music of the Spheres*, Abacus, London, 1995.

B. Mandelbrot. *The Fractal Geometry of Nature*, W. H. Freeman, New York, 1982.

Suggested further reading

Plato. *The Republic*, Penguin, 1955.

John Strohmier, Peter Westbrook. *Divine Harmony: The Life and Teachings of Pythagoras*, Berkeley Hills Books, 1999.

CHAPTER 6
EMPIRICAL ROME

Vitruvius the architect

The natural world turns in cycles and our present situation is, more or less, a repeat pattern of the circumstances that occurred in the first century BC when Roman architect and engineer Marcus Vitruvius Pollio, known simply as Vitruvius, wrote *The Ten Books on Architecture*, which is recognised as one of the great classical works of antiquity and perhaps the Western world's most important book on the subject. The book includes aspects of the design of houses, temples and cities; the classical orders; dowsing for water; the proportions of the human body to be reflected in the design of buildings; and the design and 'musical tuning' of war machines and methods to thwart enemy attack in fortifications. There is also the technique for amplifying sound in theatres using bronze urns and water.

Vitruvius attributed the decline in the quality of architecture and the poor choice of sites to architects being distracted by peripheral indulgences and their lack of education in the arts, sciences and the fundamental principles of design. He also knew there was little point in trying to get architects and their tutors to respect the fundamental principles handed down from the healer-priest builders who were the masters of ancient wisdom and the natural laws, or canon, of the universe.

Significantly, Vitruvius addressed the book directly to Augustus Caesar, the emperor of Rome, who had recently returned from successful campaigns abroad and was about to commence an extensive programme of new buildings and cities. Throughout the book, Vitruvius constantly refers to the emperor to remind the reader that it is the knowledge of the well-informed client, rather than the architect and tutors alone, which has the power to influence and effect changes that improve the quality of the buildings and enrich the lives of the citizens of Rome – something that is as pertinent to twenty-first century patrons and clients as it was 2,000 years ago.

In a most forthright manner, Vitruvius told the emperor that if he wanted excellence he had to become a well-informed patron – or client – who would understand the prerequisite qualities to be found in a good architect. Therefore, before commissioning any architects, Caesar should ensure they met the appropriate polymath standards of knowledge, understanding and skills in philosophy, science and the art of architecture:

> [An architect] ought, therefore, to be both naturally gifted and amenable to instruction [...] let him be educated, skilful with a pencil, instructed in geometry, know much about history, have followed the philosophers with attention, understood music, have some knowledge of medicine, know the opinions of jurists, and be acquainted with astronomy and the theory of the heavens [...and] *all these subjects have a common bond and union of intercourse with one another.* (Italics mine.)

Drawing skills   Before CAD (computer-aided design) became affordable, student architects were expertly taught the skills of freehand drawing. Using a pencil to draw and study the human body, a leaf or plant, created a kinaesthetic awareness that can heighten an understanding of organic structure and natural growth.

Geometry   Geometry is number in form or space. Using only a straight edge and compass, the plane, solid and spatial geometry of Euclid and Pythagoras can be produced as a philosophical discipline of profound meaning as well as having a practical purpose in building and engineering.

History   The history of architecture measures the history of humankind and the perpetuation of perennial wisdom. The subject is usually taught in the early student years but is often downgraded as anachronistic and of little importance to today's culture. Student architects might be interested to know why there is a water stream precisely located under the altar in cathedrals; or why tall, ancient pagodas survive earthquakes when all other buildings have collapsed – the simple technology was incorporated into the high-rise Mitsubishi Corporation offices in Marunouchi Park, Tokyo (Appendix 2); or why the thousand-year-old nightingale floor in Kyoto's Nijo Castle still works as a burglar alarm system (Appendix 3); or that Vitruvius used water-filled urns to amplify sound in a theatre. The study of history could also point the way towards reducing our increasing dependency on electronic technology.

Philosophy   In Vitruvius' time, and before the Age of Enlightenment, philosophy included science, physics and metaphysics. One of the keys to understanding the architecture of Chartres Cathedral lies in the west front's prominent sculptures of Pythagoras, Euclid, Boethius and Ptolemy.

Music   Keys, harmonic ratios and proportions are the basis and essence of music throughout nature and the natural world. Vitruvius referred to a building's key as a determination of its proportions, dimensions, shapes and volumes just as a composer of music selects a specific key for a new work. The choice is determined by the desired emotional effect. Eighteen centuries later, Goethe cited architecture as frozen music. (Appendix 4)

Medicine   The architect should also have knowledge of the study of medicine on account of questions of climates, air, the healthiness and unhealthiness of sites, and the use of different waters. For without these considerations, the healthiness of a dwelling cannot be assured. Four hundred years before Vitruvius was born, Hippocrates produced detailed observations on diet, breakdowns in bodily processes and the ways in which natural and built environments affect our health and the quality of life.

The jurists   As for legal matters, architects are now so overwhelmed by codes, rules, regulations, by-laws and bureaucracy that far too much valuable time and effort must be spent in conformance and avoiding litigation rather than designing buildings.

Cosmology   The proportions of the human body reflect a divine will, so the proportions of architecture should reflect the order of the cosmos. According to Vitruvius, 'Still, the observation that all studies have a common bond of union and intercourse with one another, will lead to the belief that this can be easily realised.' He acknowledged that architects could not be expected to become expert practitioners in every field, but they should nevertheless have a good working knowledge and understanding of these subjects as well as the practical building business of budgets, fees, legalities, materials, construction techniques, sustainability, protection and functional space.

Eventually, Caesar the client listened: 'I found Rome a city of bricks,' Caesar Augustus said, 'and left it as a city of marble.'

In an article in *The Times* in 2019, Mark Bridge reported on recent research published in *Physics World* in which French engineers and academics were studying cloaking devices that could deploy geometric barriers to channel electromagnetic or other seismic energy waves to protect buildings from earthquake damage. They had discovered that Greeks and Romans used advanced anti-seismic engineering that resembled modern metamaterials. These design techniques preserved ancient buildings such as the Parthenon, the Coliseum and other great works of antiquity built on or near quake-prone fault lines. Bridge says, 'Advanced anti-seismic engineering may have to be added to sanitation, medicine, education, wine, public order, irrigation and the rest in the list of what the Romans did for us.'

Researchers at Imperial College and South America's Regional Initiative for Hydrological Monitoring of Andean Ecosystems have discovered that pre-Inca technology, which dates back 1,400 years, could provide a solution to Peru's unstable water system. The region is overwhelmed by rainwater in the wet season and in short supply during the dry season. The ancient irrigation system created a network through the mountains to divert excess water that resurfaced a few weeks later. Dr Boris Ochoa-Tocachi, who led the study, said, 'With the advent of modern science, you'd be forgiven for wondering how ancient methods could apply to modern-day problems. However, it turns out that we have lots to learn from our ancestors' creative problem-solving skills.'

Works cited

Vitruvius. *The Ten Books on Architecture,* Dover Publications, 1960.

Mark Bridge. 'How the rise of quake-proofing stopped fall of Roman Empire', *The Times*, 17 June 2019.

Rozina Sabur. 'Pre-Inca technology could help solve Lima's growing water shortage', *The Telegraph*, 26 June 2019.

CHAPTER 7
THE MEDIEVAL AGES

The healer-priest architects and Chartres Cathedral

Chartres Cathedral is, perhaps, the finest example of the perennial wisdom of mystery school teachings in the West. It is likely the healer-priest architects of the school of Chartres were Knights Templar Neo-Platonists who were initiate masters of esoteric mysticism. The creed of the Neo-Platonist school combined tenets of Christianity that did not accept Christ was a man on the cross, hence the absence in the cathedral of any sculptures depicting the crucifixion. Their knowledge embraced a philosophy of matter, spirit and the soul that was generated by the laws of the cosmos. The architects of Chartres Cathedral created one of the world's most intriguing, enigmatic expressions of the transcendental language of symbolism, embedded in the location, numbers, geometry, construction and the very fabric of the building, the decoration and the sculptures. Here there is no 'art for art's sake' – every form and element of Chartres has a practical significance as well as being an expression of covert mystical knowledge.

The provincial, self-contained town of Chartres lies on the great plain of Beauce, about fifty miles west of Paris. The cathedral stands in the centre of the town on a slight mound.

Below it is an ancient maze of caverns, a grotto and spring about thirty metres (100 feet) or so beneath the crypt. The rural countryside, littered with Megalithic stone circles, obelisks and dolmens, marks the locality as an ancient site of cultural significance and positive Earth energy fields. Centuries before the Christian era, Chartres was an important shrine for Celtic pilgrims and others who came from far afield in the East, making extremely hazardous journeys to bathe in the shrine's healing waters and spend time in the grotto in prayer and penance. A Romanesque basilica, built over the older ruins above the grotto, was destroyed by fire in the eleventh century, and the building of the new church was also destroyed by fire. In 1194 the devoted people of the town began the awesome task of rebuilding the cathedral that now stands. It was consecrated in 1260. Chartres is one of several Gothic cathedrals in the region dedicated to Notre Dame. The cathedrals form a pattern on the ground that mirrors the constellation of Venus – the Virgin – in order to symbolise a heavenly paradise, a 'City of Jerusalem' on Earth.

The etheric foundation of the cathedral was established by a point precisely over the power centre of the site. This point is like the Hindu *bindu* – the seed from which the whole building is generated and manifested. The cathedral's geometric keys and symbolic dedications were set by priest-architects who directed the generations of master masons who worked on the building. The master masons were initiated into the secret knowledge that enabled them to translate the metaphysical master plan into a physical reality. The harmonic wholeness of the cathedral is not only aesthetically fulfilling – the eye subliminally senses the coordination – but the body also responds to the resonance of its proportions. The ear can readily hear the ethereal acoustic qualities that are registered by the musical scale corresponding to the heights of the vaultings.

Chartres does not follow the earlier tradition of aligning the building on a precise north-south and east-west axis. The apparently arbitrary orientation of 46° 54' to the north-east was determined by the natural magnetic veins known as 'snake currents' or 'dragon lines' that follow the line of subterranean water from the grotto well to locate the nave, or spiritual centre of the church, over the spring. Where the cathedral's nave and chancel, choir and chapels are 'bent', they have been aligned with subtle geodetic, subterranean patterns to avoid disturbance to the existing positive Earth energies and radiating streams below.

The clues for deciphering the master geometric harmonic key of Chartres Cathedral are found on the central entrance to the south doorway. The elongated statue of Christ holds a sacred book, which is a golden section rectangle, and the statue of St John is also holding a book in the proportion of 2:1. The key ensured that every piece of stone conformed to the same proportions and ratios as the whole structure of the building. On the west front Royal Portal are prominent statues that pay homage to ancient philosophers. Plato's seven liberal arts are represented by the trivium sculptures of Donat and Priscian (grammarians), Aristotle (dialectic or logic) and Cicero (rhetoric). The quadrivium is represented by the sculptures of Euclid, the founder of Greek geometry handed down from the esoteric schools of ancient Egypt; Pythagoras, master of geometry, ethics, mathematics, metaphysics and his music of the spheres; Ptolemy, the Greco-Roman, mathematician, astrologer and geographer; and Boethius, the Roman philosopher and translator of the ancient Greek philosophers.

The different relative heights of the two towers on the west front have a dimensional correlation with the geometry and lengths in the nave. Atop the northern spire is the sign of the Sun, symbolically representing Christ; the southern, lower tower bears the sign of the Moon, representing the feminine principle – the Virgin Mary. Other references to astrology are the four fixed signs representing earth, water, fire and air that are carved on the lectern in the nave. (In most medieval church architecture, there are usually some references to the zodiac and the four gospels: for example, the bull (Taurus), the fish (Pisces), the eagle (Scorpio) and a man (Aquarius))

According to Professor Keith Critchlow, the west front façade bears another unusual resemblance to the Hindu chakra system of energy centres. On the west front there are four pillars; ten panes of glass between the mullions of the tall windows; twelve roundels and ovals of glass in the great circular window; sixteen arches with inset figures above the window and two figures on either side of the Virgin. It seems unlikely these correspondences are mere coincidence.

Each of the magnificent stained-glass windows reminds the worshippers of the teachings of Christ. The labyrinth was located close to the west front entrance so that worshippers could traverse the 'pilgrims' way' before approaching the altar. If the great west window (the cosmic wheel of eternal spirit) were folded down 90° on to the nave it would cover the same area as the labyrinth representing the pathway or journey of the soul.

Whatever the weather, be it dull or sunny, from dawn to dusk, Chartres Cathedral is always bathed in an otherworldly opalescent spectre of light that glazes the nave's stone floor. Most of the original glass remains intact, but where small panels have been replaced with modern pieces, the light shining on the floor is dappled with tiny patches of blue, red or white. No one has yet discovered the secret of replicating the stained glass, said to have come from the alchemists of ancient Persia.

Chartres is the organic manifestation of universal esoteric teachings that stretch back thousands of years. When a building is designed according to the fundamental laws of geometry and music, it will resonate with the natural geometric proportions of the human body and enhance our experience so that we feel connected in time and space and in tune with the natural world about us.

Suggested further reading

Titus Burckhardt. *Chartres and the Birth of the Cathedral*, Golgonoonza Press, Ipswich, 1995.

Louis Charpentier. *The Mysteries of Chartres Cathedral*, Rilko Books, London, 1982.

CHAPTER 8
THE RENAISSANCE

The polymath architects

Filippo Brunelleschi (1377–1446), the founder of Renaissance architecture, was trained as a goldsmith and took up architecture later in life after studying Roman remains and Roman building techniques. Leon Battista Alberti (1404–72) was a scholar, author, musician, mathematician and athlete who studied ancient Roman builders and their principles of design and treated architecture as an intellectually disciplined social act, requiring skills in painting and mathematics. He was the first to 'design at a distance'. Leonardo da Vinci (1452–1519) was a painter, sculptor, inventor, engineer, biologist, botanist and geologist who designed buildings but had no training to be an architect.

In 1556, Daniele Barbaro, Venetian architect, historian, philosopher and mathematician, and friend of Andrea Palladio, translated Vitruvius' treatise, *The Ten Books on Architecture*, which had been lost for 1,500 years. He published it in Latin and Italian versions – *Vitruvii de Architectura Libri Decem/I dieci libri dell'architettura di M. Vitruvio*. It remained the bible for architects, painters and scholars until the late nineteenth and early twentieth centuries when it came to be regarded as anachronistic and of little import in a new world of technology and modern enlightenment. Together with Plato's seven liberal arts, Vitruvius' treatise was a significant influence on the lives and works of all the great Renaissance architects, scholars and painters such as Michelangelo, Leonardo da Vinci, and others, who in turn, influenced Western art and culture for the next five hundred years.

In England, Andrea Palladio (1508–80) trained to be a stonemason and is considered to be one of the great architects and most initiated of the period. His book *I quattro libri dell'architettura* (The Four Books of Architecture) illustrates his design philosophy of incorporating the divine harmonic proportions of antiquity. Each project would be assigned a proportional key, such as 1:2 (octave) or 3:2 (fifth) or 4:3 (fourth), depending on what mood or spirit Palladio wished to invoke. Each architectural drawing would be inscribed with the key – such as 3:2 – for that particular building design, including the landscape, setting, plans, sections, elevations and interior design, to ensure that assistants working on a specific project would be left in no doubt as to the proportional ratio basis of the whole concept. The building was thus *tuned* according to the Pythagorean musical harmonic proportions. Palladio also recommended seven volumes for rooms that were most appropriate for the mood or state of mind. Each example described the method for designing the most harmonious length and width of the heights related to the plan of the room. (Appendix 4)

Inigo Jones (1573–1652), a contemporary of Shakespeare, was a painter, festival designer and masque maker, an antiquarian and military engineer. He used the double cube as the key for the design of Wilton House, England. Although he was educated as an Elizabethan, he introduced Palladian-style Renaissance architecture to Britain and created some of the finest buildings of the period. Sir Christopher Wren (1632–1723), physicist, astronomer, mathematician and founder of the Royal Society, regarded architecture as a hobby. He was influenced by French and Italian baroque styles. In addition to St Paul's Cathedral, he built fifty-one churches, thirty-six company halls and the Greenwich hospital, and was probably England's most successful baroque architect.

Sir John Vanbrugh (1664–1726), soldier, playwright and theatrical designer, became another famous architect. His contemporary, Sir Isaac Newton (1642–1727), was not only a great scientist, President of the Royal Society and Warden of the Mint, he was also an astrologer and Neo-Platonist, and wrote a million words on the philosophy of alchemy. Like the architects who preceded him, Newton too was searching for the holy grail that would resolve the interaction between the cosmos – heavenly bodies – and the materiality on Earth.

Rudolf Wittkower, the twentieth-century historian, commenting on Daniele Barbaro's views, that the fundamental principles of architecture are *ordinatio* (order), concerning the measure of each element and part of the building, from the macrocosmic movement and dimensions of the celestial bodies to the microcosm of life on Earth, including subatomic structures. He believed that they are all *ordered* according to proportional relationships found in number, geometry and music and where these universal ratios correspond there will be goodness, beauty and truth: *dispositio* (arrangement), *decor* (propriety) and *distributio* (economy) are putting things in their right places with an elegance generated from the plan, elevation and perspective.

Regarding proportions, Wittkower said, 'The proportions of the human body are consonant and harmonious like the chords of a guitar. Of singers it is expected that their voices should be in tune, and the same applies to the parts in architecture. This beautiful manner in music as well as in architecture is called harmony, mother of grace and of delight.'

In other words, architectural arrangement is like musical composition: first, the composer selects the key of a symphony and then 'designs' all the multiple variations of notes, chords, melody and timing consistent with harmonic ratios within the discipline of that specific musical key. In his book, *Geometry, Proportion and the Art of Lutherie: A study of the use and aesthetic significance of geometry and numerical proportion in the design of European bowed and plucked string instruments in the sixteenth, seventeenth and eighteenth centuries*, Kevin Coates refers to Vitruvius as master and guide in the study of the use of the aesthetic significance of geometry and numerical proportion in the design of lutherie. A modern piano has five black and eight white notes making the thirteen notes of an octave, a completed chromatic scale. The arrangement conforms to the fundamental rule of the Fibonacci series, the geometric key for the golden section. Pythagoras' music of the spheres described how the geometric orbital patterns of the heavenly bodies follow the same harmonic ratios found in musical progressions.

Until the last few decades of the twentieth century, the *Vitruvii de Architectura Libri Decem* had been obligatory study – especially the classical orders – for all student architects. Now there may be only a very few, if any, schools of art and architecture where, even out of historic interest alone, the master works of say, Vitruvius, Pythagoras and Plato are not dismissed as anachronistic and irrelevant to the modern world.

Renaissance architects were inspired to draw a direct connection between the proportions of the human body and the proportions of an ideal building. When the Royal Academy of Arts established the professional training of architects in 1770, its first professor of architecture, Thomas Sandby, said, 'It is, above all things, necessary that the young student should, as early as possible, habituate himself to the story of the sublime and beautiful [...and] the stupendous works of nature.' Drawing the golden section spiral of a nautilus shell, and the Platonic polyhedrons representing the five classical elements of earth, air, fire, water and ether, has a value and practical purpose in buildings and engineering.

Fast-forward to the twenty-first-century schools of architecture and many student architects are taught neither the skills of freehand drawing nor how to manually set out an exterior or interior perspective; neither is skiagraphy taught, the study and science of shadows, which are vital tools for the design of buildings and cities. Manual drawing skills encourage perceptions that will not be experienced by staring at a computer screen.

Renaissance art and science could be defined by the three arch polymaths of Marsilio Ficino (1433–1499), the Florentine philosopher Leonardo da Vinci (1452–1519) and the English occult philosopher John Dee (1527–1608). Marsilio Ficino was one of the most prodigious writers and philosophers of the early Renaissance. He translated the complete works of Plato and the metaphysical, humanist liberal arts. He was a scholar, doctor of medicine, musician, astrologer and priest who believed 'the dignity of Man was not only reflected in architecture and art but had to be expressed in every field of human activity'. Ficino was the mentor of Lorenzo de' Medici, Alberti, Michelangelo, Raphael, Titian et al who embodied the Renaissance and influenced the intellectual, social and political forces of Europe.

Leonardo da Vinci, the 'universal genius', was an accomplished musician. According to Neil Fisher, writing in *The Times* to mark da Vinci's quincentenary, music was placed 'on top of the arts' and was 'the shaping of the invisible'. It aligned the proportion of the human figure with musical harmonics and the receding ratios of perspective as a form of musical progressions.

John Dee taught Euclidian geometry and influenced the emerging class of technical craftsmen and artisans. He was an expert on navigation, astrology, astronomy, mathematics, alchemy, medicine and philosophy, and an adviser to Elizabeth I. Shakespeare's Prospero in *The Tempest* may have been based on him.

In 1610, the Society of the Rosicrucian Order published its tenet that the material arts and sciences were a reflection of divine wisdom and that only by penetrating the inner secrets of nature could human beings achieve understanding and appreciate reality based on the eternal doctrine of Neo-Platonism and Hebrew and Hindu theology. Sir Christopher Wren and many other notables were members of the Order. Their belief in classical esotericism and the mystical concept of a unified, interconnected, harmonious cosmos embracing the whole of existence as living, vibrating energy, expressed in scholarship, art and architecture, continued until Newtonian science and physics became disassociated from philosophy and metaphysics.

Works cited

Vitruvius (trans. Daniele Barbaro). *I dieci libri dell'architettura di M. Vitruvio*, Venice, Marcolini, 1556.

Andrea Palladio. *The Four Books of Architecture,* Dover Publications, 1965.

Rudolf Wittkower. *Architectural Principles in the Age of Humanism*, University of California Press, 1972.

Kevin Coates. *Geometry, Proportion and the Art of Lutherie,* Clarendon Press, Oxford, 1985.

Neil Fisher. 'Leonardo da Vinci as you've never heard him', *The Times*, 6 April 2019.

Suggested further reading

Keith Critchlow. *Order in Space*, Thames & Hudson, London, 1997.

Robert Lawlor. *Sacred Geometry: Philosophy & Practice*, Thames & Hudson, London, 1982.

Joy Hancox. *The Byrom Collection*, Jonathan Cape, London, 1972.

CHAPTER 9

THE AGE OF ENLIGHTENMENT

The gentleman architects

Major social and political changes and increasing population growth followed the late-seventeenth century's development of the Agricultural Revolution and the early beginnings of the Industrial Revolution in Britain. The Age of Enlightenment is said to have begun with the 1687 publication of Sir Isaac Newton's *Philosophiae Naturalis Principia Mathematica*. The book detonated an explosion of the printed word and a booming interest in philosophy, the arts, music and science. Wealthy dilettantes embarked on the Grand Tour of Europe to explore the archaeology and roots of Western culture's architecture. Many became the gentlemen architects who influenced the styles of the next three hundred years, ranging from Regency terraces, neoclassicism and neo-Gothicism to the Romantic movement and ending with the twentieth century's Modernism.

Running parallel with the nostalgia for antiquity, the eighteenth century's philosophical and cultural revolutions established the supreme reign of science, logic and rationality. It was an age that repudiated the existence of the spirit of the human psyche because, under a microscope, it could not be analysed or dissected. Neither would it have revealed that we are highly sensitive organisms, constantly reacting to the minute external vibrations that influence our actions, thought processes and every other aspect of our daily life. Since then, only the physical body has been addressed. Orthodox science does not readily recognise the holistic, subtle, multi-dimensions of human beings and all living organisms, including those of planet Earth.

> When men lack a sense of awe, there will be
> disaster. (Lao Tzu, Tao Te Ching, chapter 72)

Western culture's well-established scepticism of anything neither logical nor scientifically proven has tended to sever or suppress a part of our innate sense and awareness of nature and natural surroundings. The ethos of materialism and mechanism has led to an eroded and isolated culture in which everything appears to be reduced to time, space and quantity. In other words, materiality obscures the human soul and the *why* of living is ignored.

Materialism was not a new concept. As early as the fourth century BC, Democritus called his mechanistic theory of nature and the universe *Atomism*, which, incidentally, coincided with Hippocrates breaking away from holistic healing therapies to create allopathic medicine. (Materialism and logic impelled the marine architects who designed and constructed the *Titanic* to provide lifeboats for only half the number on board, because the ship was unsinkable. More than 1,500 lives were lost.)

The two best-selling books published in 1776 were the Scottish philosopher Adam Smith's *The Wealth of Nations* and historian Edward Gibbon's *The History of the Decline and Fall of the Roman Empire.* The one expounded the controversies of the Industrial Revolution and the influence of economics on government policies. The other traced the development of Western culture and civilisation. Paradoxically, the teaching of art, metaphysics, humanistic philosophy, literature, physics and science became pigeonholed and compartmentalised into separate disciplines that fragmented their integral common bond. This laid the foundation for the nineteenth century's divisions of professional institutions and became an unintended source of the marginalisation of the practice of architecture today.

Philosophical and political differences marked the turbulent conflicts of the final quarter of the eighteenth century. The Boston Tea Party (just one of the many versions of a Brexit throughout history) triggered colonial Americans' War of Independence that ended in 1783. Six years later, the French Revolution and the rise of Napoleon erupted in Europe. It could be said that two books by the same British-American author, Thomas Paine, exacerbated and accelerated the end of the Age of Enlightenment. His *Rights of Man*, published in 1791, argued that 'popular political revolution is permissible when a government does not safeguard the natural rights of people'. (Now there's something for all leaders and politicians to think about while they're talking.) Three years later, he published *The Age of Reason: Being an Investigation of True and Fabulous Theology*, which set off another challenge to the establishment.

A. C. Grayling's recent book, *The History of Philosophy*, clarifies the current meaning of the word 'philosophy'. Throughout history, until the Enlightenment, it meant general enquiry and science; a philosopher was someone who investigated anything and everything. Since the nineteenth century, philosophy and science have become compartmentalised and divergent. Today, philosophy includes metaphysics, ethics, logic, epistemology, politics and language; and science is a separate, specialised, technical discipline.

The defeat of Napoleon, and the pace of the agricultural and industrial revolutions surging ahead, marked in Britain the early nineteenth century's new Victorian era.

Work cited

A. C. Grayling. *The History of Philosophy*, Penguin Viking, 2019.

CHAPTER 10
THE AGE OF DEMARCATION

The professional architects

The 1837 coronation of Queen Victoria coincided with the foundation of the RIBA and the establishment of other professional institutions: the Royal Institution of Chartered Surveyors (RICS); the Institution of Civil Engineers (ICE); the Institution of Electrical Engineers (IEE); the Chartered Institute of Building (CIOB); the British Medical Association (BMA); and the various trade unions (firemen, bakers, train drivers, printers et al).

According to the historian Niall Ferguson, 'A civilisation is defined more by its institutions than the buildings where they are housed or indeed the faith or ideology that inspires them.' Demarcation limits boundaries of influence, interest and activity. The culture of the polymath faded away and 'Jack-of-all-trades' became a disparaging epithet. 'Demarcation' is the byword that trade unions use to justify industrial strike action. Separation and the compartmentalisation of the professions, trades and working practices remain overshadowed in today's twenty-first century. Socially, we still identify ourselves by our lifetime specialised occupations and through to retirement and beyond. When introduced to a stranger, usually the first question is, 'What do you do?' Imagine how a polymath such as a Leonardo da Vinci or a John Dee would have responded.

Demarcation significantly fosters 'That's not my job' syndrome and anything outside the scope of a profession's specific expertise is considered to be the interest, research and business of others.

Victorian England was literally awash, with streets and rivers overflowing with raw sewage, unpiped water and the severe overcrowding of urban buildings. A typhus epidemic in 1838 marked the first time in British history that doctors were employed to look at the sanitary conditions that might have contributed to the ill health of the population.

In 1839, reformer Sir Edwin Chadwick researched the appalling unsanitary conditions of 'the labouring population' of Great Britain. Following his extensive crusade, together with the Towns Association, the government was forced in 1848 to introduce the first of the Public Health Acts. Later, Chadwick's campaigns would rely heavily on Florence Nightingale's documented reports on the 1853–1856 Crimean War. She had led a party of nurses to work in military hospitals where ten times more soldiers were dying of disease than battle wounds. When she reduced overcrowding, improved the sewerage system, increased the natural light and ventilation, and created a calm atmosphere with views of nature and the natural world, the death rate of forty-two per cent was reduced to two per cent and a return to health. (Sunlight therapy to kill off tuberculosis (TB) bacteria was used at a clinic founded by Swiss doctor Auguste Rollier in 1903. Two years later, when he presented his findings at a medical conference in Paris, the entire audience walked out in disbelief. No surprise there then.) Eventually, with the consolidated Public Health Act 1875, the government took responsibility for the health of its citizens.

Since Chadwick's first published reports of 1839, it appears that Victorian architects and engineers were either unaware of, or disinterested in, improving environmental conditions in Britain. Evidence for all to experience, including architects, was the Big Stink of 1858 and 1859 when the putrid smell from the sewage in the Thames kept people away from the bridges. Even the new middle-class houses were defective, with fungus, moisture-laden walls and poor drainage systems.

The problem in Britain in the first half of the nineteenth century was that there were no building codes. The problem in the twentieth century was the emphasis on the training and the practice of architecture to focus on designing wind and weathertight buildings of whatever style, which would be in full conformance with local and national building codes. This did not tend to encourage architects and their clients to investigate other areas that might have negative impacts on the design of the built environment. One such serious health hazard in buildings was, and still is, radon gas.

An account of the effects of what is known as radon gas first appeared in 1556 in *De Re Metallica* by Georgius Agricola. He had studied mining in central Europe and discovered many miners were dying a painful death from rotting lungs caused by breathing in the pestilential air. Improved ventilation shafts and the use of lace face masks helped to reduce the mortality rate. The subject became noticed in 1920 when it was identified by British researchers as radon (Rn), a heavy, radioactive, colourless, odourless and tasteless gas that naturally occurs in the Earth's crust in various regions and levels throughout the world. The gas is a highly cancerous health risk that will penetrate concrete and brickwork, and seep through pipe fissures, and is present in many ordinary building materials in everyday use such as plasterboards, blocks and granite bricks.

This information was public knowledge for sixty-five years before radon legislation was included in UK building codes in 1985. During this period, neither the government nor the professions took action to design and construct their buildings to treat and prevent gas penetration until the by-laws demanded conformance. Currently, it is estimated that radon causes an annual death toll of 1,100 citizens from lung cancer in the UK alone.

In addition to radon, there are several other site health hazards such as weak electromagnetic and Earth energy fields that bygone master architects understood and took preventive action to mitigate. They also knew how to harness positive, health-enhancing subterranean forces.

In the 1960s, 2,000 years after Vitruvius set out a number of design techniques for the protection of the city and its citizens, a group of innovative architects, criminologists and police officers published their concept for crime prevention through environmental design (CPTED) – also known as defensive space – to create safer environments and improve quality of life. There is little evidence that schools of architecture and practising professionals have addressed the link between architectural design and planning with security and crime prevention, and yet the UK crime rate has risen and the threat of terrorism is now ever-present.

The 1998 Crime and Disorder Act imposes a duty of care on local authorities, their planning committees and architects to assist in the prevention of crime and the fear of crime. It is not specifically mentioned in the ARB's teaching curriculum, but its current code of conduct does require the security of electronic and paper records and data protection to be safeguarded. How many architects incorporate the CPTED concepts in their built environment strategies and designs?

Throughout history, even master architects have ignored the needs of those who have some form of physical handicap. It wasn't until 1995 that the Disability Discrimination Act (DDA) became law and forced the profession to incorporate design features to address the hazards and difficulties of the twenty per cent of the population who are disabled. Was it indifference, apathy, unawareness or myopic vision that allowed the needs of the 13.9 million currently disabled people in the UK to slip between the demarcated and compartmentalised responsibilities of professional architects, medical practitioners, social services and government departments?

Prior to the 1995 Act, the single exception of an architect addressing disability occurred in 1934 when Berthold Lubetkin designed a series of ramps for the physically challenged penguins in their pool at London Zoo.

The post-war transition

When a journalist asked what was most likely to blow a government off course, prime minister Harold Macmillan famously replied, 'Events, dear boy, events.' During the 1945 post-war years, external events and existentialism blew the practice of architecture off course. Bombing in London, Coventry and other major towns and cities had decimated whole communities where a sense of belonging and neighbourliness had once thrived. The often unnecessary, but socially expedient, slum clearance programmes added to the fragmentation and isolation created by the extensive building of stark, tarmacked housing estates.

There was extreme austerity and political stress and unrest: materials were licensed; there was a three-day week. Home secretary George Brown banned office building; there was the miners' strike; the Cold War; and the over-powerful unions. (Businesses that needed telephones were at the mercy of the union barons who ran the General Post Office (GPO) until it became British Telecom (BT).

Shortages and restrictions were exacerbated in Britain by the introduction of the 1947 Town and Country Planning Acts giving local authorities powerful legislation to control building development. Property clients tended to appoint the practices most likely to squeeze the greatest volume of building development out of a site rather than commission those with a reputation for their other valued qualities as architects. Successful practices often knew as much, if not more, town planning law than local planning officers did.

Generally, post-war unemployment was high in the UK. About fifty per cent of the profession had to find permanent work in local authorities' architect departments. (That number is now reduced to nine per cent). Private practices thrived by balancing a mix of new projects with rebuilding bombed sites and repairing or refurbishing existing buildings.

In the 1960s, the City of London, also known as the Square Mile, began to develop into the financial and banking centre of the world. International banks flocked to the UK to establish a representative office in the City. During the following ten years these significant changes led to the 1972 redevelopment of Docklands and the derestriction of the rigid policy of conservation, which meant that site assembly for new offices was now permitted. Despite encountering additional investment pressures and controls, enterprising practices ventured to explore the potential of new business in Europe and the Middle East.

Works cited

Niall Ferguson. 'Scorched but standing – two symbols of the West', *The Sunday Times*, 21 April 2019.

Suggested further reading

Thomas Saunders. *The Boiled Frog Syndrome*, Wiley-Academy, 2002, (radon pp 17–19).

Richard H. Schneider, Ted Kitchen. *Planning for Crime Prevention*, Routledge, London, 2002.

CHAPTER 11
THE AGE OF GLOBALISATION

The transition architects

Globalisation, climate change and reaction to the design of dystopian environments define the twenty-first century. An event in 1983 in the City of London, called the Big Bang, marked the deregulation of finance and the development of business computerisation. It created an emerging global demand for multi-storey, air-conditioned buildings with large, open floor plans and advanced building technology. Whatever the prevailing climate and environmental factors, offices, hotels, hospitals and certain vast sports stadia are air conditioned. Even in private homes in temperate climates, air conditioning is no longer considered a luxury but a lifestyle necessity.

Air conditioning is global warming's Catch 22: warmer global temperatures lead to more air conditioning and more air conditioning leads to rising global temperatures and rising peak electricity use resulting in overload and blackouts. According to a report by Stephen Buranyi in the *Guardian* in 2019, 'The IEA [International Energy Agency] projects that as the rest of the world reaches similar levels, air conditioning will use about 13% of all electricity worldwide, and produce 2bn tonnes of CO_2 a year – about the same as India, the world's third largest emitter, produces today.' In 2018, fifty per cent of Beijing's power capacity was due to air conditioning.

An increasing number of doctors and scientists are now expressing deep concerns about future wireless technology, which poses a bigger threat than global warming. It is considered one of the most pressing environmental health hazards, needing architects to take a leading role to exercise, whenever possible, the prudent avoidance of electromagnetic pollution.

Dr Nyjon Eccles heads a Harley Street clinic called the Natural Doctor, which specialises in integrative medicine. In an article on his website, he writes:

> [We are] saturated with coverage of deep concerns about the fate of the planet, of national security, of climate change and more besides[…] [But] we have managed to overlook the biggest threat of all […] that 5G technology poses to human, plant and animal health. […] [Recently] more than 230 prominent and highly regarded doctors and scientists from more than 40 countries have signed the 5G Appeal […] to halt the roll-out of 5G due to serious concerns about the impact it will have on health. 5G on paper will have the power to run the world. Literally. Driverless cars, integrated road systems, instant data transfer, […] military systems […] The price? Greater infrastructure. More receivers, more satellites and more radio frequency electromagnetic fields (RF-EMF) that is the greatest threat yet to global health.

Following a report from its risk assessment team in 2010, Lloyds of London, the world's largest insurer, is refusing to cover claims against the new 5G cellphone network, likening it to the asbestos scandal.

Several countries, including France, ban all cell towers and Wi-Fi from elementary school premises to reduce the effect of radiation and the rise in cancer cases in young children. The Karolinska Institute in Stockholm has a long history of research into these negative health effects and reports that, as the superfast 5G cellphone network is effective only across short distances, masts will have to be installed possibly as much as one for every twelve houses in urban areas, which will massively increase EMF exposure.

All living organisms are sensitive to electromagnetic energy fields. These are the means of navigation for birds, butterflies and bees to return to their nests. Without the system of extremely weak electrical currents in our bodies, we would not be 'alive'. For the first time in the history of the planet, all living systems are exposed to unnatural biological stresses imposed by exceptionally high, artificially generated voltages and the all-pervading extremes of high and low frequencies. Other than visible light, our environment is now saturated, many million times over, by the amount of electromagnetic radiation that we experienced just a hundred years ago. Everything electric produces electromagnetic radiation and the incessant, daily increase in globally generated electromagnetic fields continues to expose everyone to levels that our bodies are unable to withstand, resulting in cancers, birth defects, skin allergies, chronic fatigue syndrome and other 'diseases of civilisation'.

We are bombarded by electromagnetic field radiation (EMR): forty per cent of the population suffers from 'mild to moderate' exposure and during the past ten years EMF pollution has increased a quintillion fold. (See *Health Hazards and Electromagnetic Fields in hospital design and equipment* by Thomas Saunders.)

An overdose of, or long-term exposure to, artificially generated electromagnetic and radio-frequency fields can produce, to a lesser or greater degree, abnormal biological changes affecting our genetic response to stress and our ability to resist disease. Awareness of the potential hazards and knowing how to avoid unnecessary exposure is the best prevention against becoming over-sensitised, but you do not necessarily have to live under overhead high-tension cables or be a prolific user of the mobile phone to suffer health impacts.

As ever, government interventions lag a long way behind public opinion and the demands for urgent action to address global warming and social changes to create life-enhancing environments. The lack of political will relinquishes the need for transition and change to the resources and consciences of others. Currently there are no government legislations in the design and installation of air conditioning except enforcing inspections to monitor efficiency and improvements. In the longer term, the best hoped-for outcome may be the use of AC units that are fifty per cent more energy-efficient but are double the cost.

However, as Stephen Buranyi noted in his *Guardian* article, there are exceptions. In 1980s Geneva, which has a warmer climate than most of America, the local government banned the installation of air conditioning other than by special permission. It is now common practice throughout Switzerland and air conditioning accounts for just two per cent of all electricity used. New York City Council passed far-reaching legislation, backed by hefty fines for offenders, requiring all large buildings in the city to reduce their emissions by forty per cent by 2030 with a goal of eighty per cent by 2050. The Council believes this is 'the largest carbon emissions reduction ever mandated by any city, anywhere'. The mayor of Los Angeles is reported to be making similar plans.

Architects need to take the initiative to address the thirty-three per cent of UK carbon emissions from the built environment. Will London's City Corporation follow suit and reduce carbon emissions for thirteen new skyscrapers already in the pipeline? Will they require architects and their developer clients to use wind tunnels and computer simulations to provide comprehensive assessments of the effects of the wind at ground level to avoid cyclists being destabilised, or pushed into the path of vehicles, by wind made worse by tall buildings in the Square Mile?

These global issues have a major impact on the training, education and practice of architecture and the whole building industry that extends beyond conformance with public health acts, planning and building codes. There is no shortage of technical know-how to be learned from nature and the traditional builders of the past to show us how to thrive even in extreme climatic conditions.

Bernard Rudofsky noted that human beings learned from beavers and apes. Architects and engineers who are interested in designing carbon-neutral buildings should study the ongoing scientific research on termite hills in the extreme climatic conditions of tropical regions. Some hills are more than 4,000 years old. These huge bioengineering mounds, as high as three metres and ten metres in diameter, are built from a 'cement' of soil mixed with water and saliva.

The constant temperature inside the mounds is maintained by a maze of tunnels and conduits of duct ways, orientated on a north-south axis, to ventilate the deep, excavated galleries of the underground nests. These 'air-conditioned' mounds act like a factory, efficiently converting carbon dioxide to oxygen.

The design of four- or eight-sided wind catchers or wind chimneys to direct air flow into private dwellings and large buildings is zero-energy, passive, natural ventilation technology that has been known since ancient Egypt. It continues to be used in many parts of the world – in desert regions, the Caribbean, West Asia, Pakistan, America, and in the UK over the past fifteen years. There are more than 7,000 public buildings using the same, unpowered wind-catcher technology, including Sir Michael Hopkins' Portcullis House, which provides offices for 213 members of Parliament.

See Chapter 15 for details on the RIBA's new 2019 Code of Conduct Professional Conduct, which has set in motion a move towards architects taking positive action and encouraging their clients to go green. The *Architizer Journal* (30 May 2019) reported that Foster & Partners have pledged to be the first practice to sign into the Net Zero Carbon Buildings Commitment launched by the World Green Building Council (WGBC). In an effort to decarbonise construction, all new buildings in the firm's portfolio will be carbon-neutral by 2030. The RIBA reported that architects signing up to the UN Climate Neutral Now initiative to reduce gas emissions must commit to calculate and disclose the carbon footprint of their projects.

The profession must also exercise prudent avoidance to reduce Wi-Fi by hard-wiring and avoiding the harmful siting of radio stations, electrical generators, substations, power lines and electrified train track. (See *Health Hazards and Electromagnetic Fields in hospital design and equipment* by Thomas Saunders.) Prudent avoidance and a changed mindset could direct architects to alternative solutions such as the nightingale floor in Kyoto, which reduces its carbon emissions to zero. (Appendix 3)

In addition to global warming and electromagnetic pollution, the third major issue is the increasing public awareness and demand for built environments to safeguard local environments and communities in order to sustain and enhance health and quality of life.

Writing in *The Times*, Sir Roger Scruton observes, 'If you ask why concepts like community, place and belonging suddenly come to occupy a central place in our politics, then you will quickly light on the fact that those aspects of the human condition are all under threat. And the threat comes from a single source: globalisation.'

Scruton is a strong opponent of what he calls the detached, global international style of architecture that is of nowhere in particular. Together with Nicholas Boys Smith, he co-chairs the Building Better, Building Beautiful Commission (BBBBC). It acts as an independent adviser to the British government to boost house building that emphasises the importance of design and its impact on local communities. A model code published in January 2020 will be the benchmark base for local councils to publish their own design code of aesthetic commitments. The model code has received a positive response from the RIBA and one trusts it will be supported by government endorsement and commitment to enforce action.

Works cited

Stephen Buranyi. 'How cold air is heating the world', *Guardian*, 29 August 2019.

Dr Nyjon Eccles. 'Is future technology a bigger threat than global warming?' thenaturaldoctor.org, 10 May 2019.

Lloyds' Risk Assessment Team. 'Electromagnetic fields from mobile phones: recent developments', lloyds.com, November 2010.

Thomas Saunders. *Health Hazards and Electromagnetic Fields in hospital design and equipment*, Elsevier Science Limited, 2003.

Roger Scruton. 'Architects turned us into citizens of nowhere', *The Times*, 20 September 2019.

PART II

THOUGHTS ON
THE PROFESSIONAL INSTITUTIONS

CHAPTER 12

THE ROYAL INSTITUTION OF CHARTERED SURVEYORS

The Royal Institution of Chartered Surveyors (RICS) was founded in 1868. Currently it has 125,000 professional members or trainees worldwide who specialise in one of its twenty-one distinct divisions – nine property groups; six land groups; and six built environment groups. All the major real estate property agents are multidisciplined, global organisations. Anyone interested in land or property matters to build, buy, sell, rent, develop, insure, value, auction, survey or with related legal issues, will likely find that their first port of call will be to a firm of chartered surveyors or someone with the suffix RICS after their name.

RICS members can offer a property client a comprehensive range of services from site availability and marketing research to advice on the preparation of the brief that specifies the shape and size of the floors, the location and treatment of the main entrance and the layout and materials for the toilets. The design brief can also determine the style and other features of the building even before an architect has been appointed. In particular, a client can be offered the services of a qualified project manager to provide a continuous representation throughout the whole development process from purchase of the site to settling the final accounts.

Many clients feel reassured to have someone 'holding their hand' to manage (control) the professional team, contractors and other stakeholders. This has encouraged clients to first appoint a project manager to develop the brief and advise on, or select the appointment of the architect and other consultants, which has contributed to the marginalisation of the role and status of the architect. This arrangement often causes discontentment when the project manager assumes a dominant gatekeeper or domineering attitude that alienates the client from the professional team. (Mention 'project manager' to an architect or contractor and watch the eyes roll heavenwards.) Of course, many property clients have their own preferred architect, consultants and project manager, but the RICS members' recommendations, introductions, goodwill and patronage are a vital and lucrative source of business for architects and others in the building industry. Chartered surveyors, even the smaller, local firms, are the godfathers of the industry.

There are extremely competent, experienced and valued project managers – some of them are even my best friends. On the other hand, the RICS offers its members a six-month distance-learning project management course of 200 hours for £1,075.00 + VAT. The 12-part syllabus is silent on matters of strategy.

A project manager acts in a managerial role as a co-ordinator and administrator. It is similar to a corporate company secretary's managerial function. The company secretary is a senior officer who manages the governance and general administration of an organisation. The role is to guide and advise the directors on compliance on all matters of company law and regulations, arrange meetings, organise agendas and distribute minutes. The company secretary provides *tactical* support to the chairman, the CEO and board of directors who are the *strategists* leading the firm. The project manager's important role is to provide tactical, administrative and compliance support to the architect, the professional team and the client. Project management is not a leadership function.

Project management, which may also include the role of construction management, is an issue in which the RIBA needs to take the lead itself to clarify, address, clearly define and publicise the difference between a member of the project team as a tactical manager and the architect as the lead consultant. Such a change to the prevailing culture will demand effective changes to the current curriculum in our schools of architecture.

CHAPTER 13
THE ARCHITECTS REGISTRATION BOARD

The Architects Registration Board (ARB) states that its purpose is to maintain public trust and confidence in the integrity of both the architects' profession and the ARB as an independent UK regulator of architects. The ARB registers and controls the use of the designation 'architect' together with its own Code of Conduct (which is not aligned with the RIBA's code). It also prescribes the curriculum for the training and education of architects and controls the qualifications and practical experience required to be registered to practice and call yourself an architect in the UK.

Five lay members of the public, five architects and one independent non-executive chairperson are the members of the ARB board selected and appointed by the Privy Council. All eleven appointed board members can choose to remain in office for up to eight years. The Privy Council are backbench members of Parliament who are appointed by their respective political parties to serve on the Select Committee of the Ministry of Housing, Communities and Local Government (MHCLG). The Ministry deals with building regulations, planning, housing and urban regeneration. (This is where the Grenfell Tower buck stops.)

In other words, ARB board members are political appointees who control and determine the specific training and education curricula for schools of architecture and graduate entry onto the UK's Registration of Architects. Only those who have had the education, training and experience to become an architect, and are on the official UK Register of Architects, are legally entitled to use the name 'architect' in business or practice.

Thomas Heatherwick, the celebrated, award-winning English sculptor, engineer, designer and architect – the Olympic cauldron, the new London Routemaster bus, the Rolling Bridge, the Vessel in New York, and architect for many internationally acclaimed, major buildings in the world – is not qualified by the ARB to be registered and use the designation 'architect'. In other words, non RIBA-qualified, polymath architects are excluded.

In August 2019, Karen Holmes, the ARB registrar and chief executive, reported that the board has devised 'a new route to provide institutions with opportunities to develop new and innovative ways of delivering qualifications in architecture'. It could be said that the changes are more about the governance of the board than updating the prescribed curriculum. In a letter addressed to 'Dear Architect', she says, in reference to communication with the client, 'You will often hold a pivotal and unique role within a project...' That expresses the ARB's mind-set about the status of the architect. If she had omitted the words 'will often', the strategic role of the architect would be positively embedded in the minds of architects and their clients.

The institution of the profession of architecture is also unique. Since the 1997 Act, the required training and education to qualify as an architect has been controlled and directed by the

ARB, an autonomous, external organisation. In the example of the RICS, its board members control the policy and processes that set out the mapping of pathways for qualifications. An internal quality assurance monitors the education providers to ensure that the quality reflects the required high standards set by the governing institution's accreditation panel. The RICS' selection of the nine members of the panel are made up of RICS staff and qualified professionals who review the programmes. Similarly, the Institution of Structural Engineers has its own Joint Board of Moderators issue broad headings and general guidelines to define and validate learning outcomes.

Architecture in the UK is also the only profession where you have to pay twice – once to be a chartered member of the RIBA and, again, to be allowed to call yourself an architect.

It is not readily apparent from a review of the biographical information and personal interests of the members of the Privy Council and the ARB's appointed board that they have the necessary and requisite knowledge, understanding and credentials to establish an appropriate curriculum for the teaching and education of our future generations of architects. The curricula details are itemised in the ARB publication, *Prescriptions of Qualifications: ARB Criteria at Parts 1, 2 and 3*. Under Clause 6.1, the EU's European Commission has the power to make whatever alterations it may deem appropriate. Each school of architecture is allowed flexibility provided the syllabus conforms to the prescribed curricula. The Prescriptions of Qualifications document requires architects to have a knowledge and understanding of the impact of 'environmental materials and strategies; the precepts of sustainable design; the needs of the building users; and the intellectual histories, theories and technologies'.

Although the ARB's practical, day-to-day business is indeed about budgets, fees, legalities, materials, construction techniques and functional space, there appears to be no specific requirement to have knowledge, understanding or awareness of the created design's impact on the human body and mind. Ecology and the environment in terms of negative Earth energy fields, electromagnetic fields, ionisation and the effect of light and shadow on endocrine glands are not specifically mentioned. Of course, architects are not expected to be expert in every field, but how does the ARB's curriculum equate with what might be considered to be the essential teaching of the fundamental values and practice of a polymath master architect that is relevant to Western civilisation?

The ARB's prescribed curriculum could be interpreted as an ideal training for architects to become well-behaved, tactical managers who will present clients with competent drawings designed to conform to current rules and regulations, and ensure they are wind and watertight buildings that are unlikely to fall down.

Today's architects, engineers and planners have focused their sights on high technology and eye-catching contemporary buildings that provide watertight sheaths to protect our material comforts without necessarily fully addressing the impact their creations have on our relationship with nature and their interconnectedness with the human psyche, health and the environment's effect on our everyday lives.

When the study and understanding of branches of the arts, sciences, philosophy, spirituality, human nature and metaphysics are compartmentalised, or not even taught, and everything is reduced to time, space and quantity, the outcome is fragmentation. The *why* of living is abandoned.

The needs of human beings extend beyond the material dimensions of physiology and biology. We are conditioned by our psychology, our psyche, our perceptions, instincts, intuitions and an awareness of the natural world, which transcend our basic requirements for simple bodily comforts and shelter from the weather.

In her recent book, *Why Architects Matter*, Professor Flora Samuel suggests, 'The profession needs to make it clear about what it knows and the value of what it knows. Without this clarity, the marginalisation of architects from the production of the built environment will continue, preventing clients, businesses and society from getting the buildings they deserve.'

Part of the answer may be that the legacy of some of the valuable and valued qualities of history's master architects are neither taught nor practised by today's architects. If so, it may be that the curriculum and validation for the training, education and practice of architecture is neither adequate nor fit for purpose.

The ARB began a review of the prescribed curriculum in 2017 and new procedures are intended to become effective in 2020. The updated version will include climate change and fire regulations (the latter in response to the deadly Grenfell Tower fire in 2017). In the meantime, the RIBA has issued a new Code of Conduct that deals with these and many other issues for architects to address that are relevant to today's pressing social, political and cultural needs.

Afterthoughts

The ARB website indicates there are sixty-one schools and institutions of architecture in the UK. The oldest independent school is the Architectural Association School of Architecture (AA) founded in 1847 by two apprenticed students, Robert

Kerr and Charles Gray, who devised a course of training instead of the usual route of being articled to an architect in practice. The AA school became formally established in 1890. Currently it remains independently unfunded by the state and draws its income and support from a yearly intake of 800 students of whom eighty per cent are non-UK. Globally, the AA is recognised as a beacon of excellence and boasts many internationally acclaimed alumni (starchitects). Its five-year diploma course in architecture is recognised and validated by the ARB and RIBA. Its 300-page prospectus, covering the whole programme from the diploma course to the graduate masters and research platforms, refers to the challenges we face today as citizens and architects:

> ...The emergence of new technologies and changing power structures, combined with growing conflicts and the ethical imperatives of our contemporaneity, make architecture today a radically exciting and challenging discipline. [The Prospectus presents] a series of pedagogical agendas and cultural programmes that articulate what architecture can contribute to the world we live in, from social, political and cultural points of view.

The AA has a rural facility in Dorset where its students can design, make and build, and handle materials. Bearing in mind that fashion design students must learn to draw and cut patterns, know stitching and the feel and qualities of materials, and student doctors have to deal with dead and living bodies, all student architects should experience say, three months of physical work on a building site, workshop or quarry – anywhere to smell, touch and feel and get their hands dirty.

2019 marked the Bauhaus centenary of the foundation of the emerging modern movement by Walter Gropius in Weimar. The school existed for fourteen years until the Nazi regime closed it down, but elements of its eclectic pedagogy are, or should be, the gold standard for the curriculum of every school of architecture. Apart from the AA, there appear to be few other schools that encourage students to be leaders, entrepreneurs, innovators and multidisciplined polymaths involved in creating a paradigm shift to evolve the role, status and value of the architect. What impact might the Bauhaus centenary have on the new RIBA and ARB curricula?

There are a number of schools of architecture turning out graduates who have neither the ability nor the inclination to draw competently with a pen or pencil. A kinaesthetic hand-eye study when manually drawing the structures of plant life or a nude body; or mechanically setting up a perspective illustration; or an exercise in skiagraphy (the projection of shadows) will equip the student with a perceptive understanding that computer graphics cannot provide. Apart from doodling as a way of triggering an inspiring thought, students and practising architects need to set themselves free from keyboards and screens. An article in *Architizer Journal* suggested that 'computer-generated renderings have their place [...] but for fluid articulation of ideas and the communication of concepts to clients, nothing beats a good old-fashioned sketch'.

Works cited

Flora Samuel. *Why Architects Matter*, Routledge, 2018.

CHAPTER 14

THE ROYAL INSTITUTE OF BRITISH ARCHITECTS

Usui civium, decori urbium/Service for the citizens and the glory of the city

Internationally renowned, the Royal Institute of British Architects (RIBA) is held in high esteem and enjoys a worldwide reputation for excellence. The Council and controlling bodies are run by and for the members who are responsible for its strategy and policies. Its governance includes the accreditation of the education and training of architects and the practice of architecture. Its by-laws and regulations cover fees and all aspects of business management, planning and building codes, budgets, project procurement and ethical conduct.

Over the past fifty years or so there have been tremors of varying magnitude that have disturbed the organisation. The 1963 introduction of business management to the Part 3 Professional Practice examinations mentioned earlier, caused a minor and positive shake-up. Ten years later, another tremor shook the RIBA's tranquillity. At the time, when about fifty per cent of architects were employed by local authorities, the RIBA was perceived to be biasedly acting as their trade union to the detriment and the expense of the other fifty per cent of the members in private practice. Subsequently, in 1973, a group of architects set up the Association of Consultant Architects (ACA), which became a well-established national, non-regulatory body. The Council is governed by councillors elected from the membership who are registered and regulated by the ARB. The ACA runs its own training and education and continuing practice development programmes. It has an independent and well-respected voice, which is solely dedicated to the interests of private practitioners.

The 5,000 members can use the ACA's own suites of standard forms of agreement and scope of services, various forms for building contracts and project partnering contracts. These address a more balanced approach to the mutual protection of architects and clients in terms of the fee structures, engagements and procurement integration, which differ from the standard RIBA documents.

The 1982 critical, far-reaching and unnecessary abandonment of the RIBA standard scale of fees has had a negative impact on architects' status and income. Clearly, the current RIBA 'recommended' fee structure is not fit for purpose. It needs to be reviewed and updated to provide an adequate scale of charges that is commensurate with architects' diverse and additional professional services, including higher fees for certain partial services. The scale should be sufficiently competent to allow every business to fulfil its duty to the clients *and* make a reasonable profit in order to serve and stay in business. Architects and clients might then treat the range of fees as minimum charges to avoid unethical, unfair competition.

In 1997, another instance of major turbulence abruptly marginalised the power and governance of the RIBA. Under a directive from the European Union, the British Parliament passed The Architects Act 1997 in order – it is understood – to address their perception of the RIBA's 'conflict of interest' as an institution run for and by its members.

The Act created the Architects Registration Board, with its own Code of Conduct. The ARB became established as an organisation, separate to and independent of the RIBA, to control and direct the training, education and practical experience for professional qualifications, as well as the registration and regulation of architects in the UK. The separation fragmented and diminished the function and role of the RIBA to one of promoting the profession and validating professional examinations. It has caused long-running conflict and resentment between the two organisations.

In 2005, the RIBA took another positive step when the new accreditation of Client Design Adviser was introduced. It encouraged clients to engage architects as independent experts to guide the strategic aspects of a project's brief and site selection in advance of the appointment of the executive architects and the project team. Unfortunately, this did nothing to improve the low socio-economic status of the profession as a whole. A further shiver occurred in 2017 when a review of the RIBA's governance by an independent firm of lawyers found 'a large number of discrepancies and structural defects'.

More recently, other specialist organisations similar to the ACA are challenging the institution of the RIBA. Offering unique niche services, they include the New London Architecture Urban Design Group and the Young Architects and Developers Alliance.

Membership

There are 44,000 UK-registered architects. They chose the job they loved and were prepared to dedicate seven years of passionate devotion, tenacity and talent to graduate and step on the lowest rung of the professional ladder. For every qualified professional there are many people from all walks of life who say they would have liked to become an architect. Approximately five per cent (2,200) of the membership work in celebrity practices run by the so-called *starchitects* – Lord Foster, Baron Richard Rogers, the late Dame Zaha Hadid, Sir Nicholas Grimshaw, Thomas Heatherwick, Renzo Piano, Frank Gehry, Skidmore, Owings & Merrill, et al. These multidisciplined, global business organisations are highly regarded and internationally eulogised in the media. They can command substantial fees. However, the majority of the membership – the ninety-five per centers (42,000) – work in practices that range from sole person to small and large-sized. Many members of this majority group experience their work as being undervalued and grossly under-rewarded for the value and services they provide. They feel marginalised, are held in low regard by the general public, and the names of a project's architects are often ignored by the media.

Have the RIBA, its members and staff, the ARB's board members and academia contributed to the erosion and dissipation of the architect's status and authority? Does the curriculum train and educate architects to understand the impact of the built environment on the human body and mind, the ecology of the planet and the value they contribute to the qualities of life?

The RIBA Council

The RIBA Council and the membership recognise that 'something must be done' to transform and improve the brand image and socio-economic status of the profession and to establish the architect as the senior consultant and strategist. It is not unusual for the new intake of RIBA Council election candidates to demand action to reform the scale of fees and address the marginalisation and low status role of architects. The manifestos could be paraphrased by a reference to Marc Antony's famous declaration in Shakespeare's *Julius Caesar*: I come to bury the RIBA, not to praise it.

However, the speech continues: 'The evil that men do lives after them; the good is often interred with their bones.' In other words, the membership might acknowledge and use the RIBA's many virtues, values and benefits it can bring to the profession and then completely discard whatever does not improve, restore and regenerate the architect's status and financial rewards. This will demand rigour to avoid the car key syndrome: in dark night-time shadows, a driver gets out of the car and drops the keys in the roadside. He/she walks about ten metres away to the street lamp to hunt for the key under the light.

What is the something that must be done to meet the challenges?

How relevant to today are these 200-year-old institutions? Architects are not alone in feeling that the RIBA – and the ARB – no longer adequately serve their profession. Many doctors feel the BMA (British Medical Association) no longer serves their medical profession; the music industry no longer serves professional musicians; politicians and their political organisations, it is often argued, no longer serve the people. Do not despair – Mandelbrot's fractals is the way of the universe: what goes around, comes around and, according to Nobel laureate José Saramago, 'Chaos is merely order waiting to be deciphered'.

Members investigating the dark side might discover a number of RIBA regulations, laws and by-laws, as well as people and their departments that do not serve the whole profession. Has the RIBA allowed the European Union to impose regulations on UK training, education and practice of architecture that are inappropriate for the UK system? Are the Council members' strategic policies being thwarted by powerful 'mandarins' – the Sir Humphrey Applebys – in the RIBA's *dark* administration and managerialism? The much needed response came in October 2019 when members voted overwhelmingly in favour of a number of changes to radically transform the governance of the institution. It also needs to transform and elevate the architect's role, status and financial reward to a level commensurate with the knowledge, value, service and practice of architecture.

The profession's prime asset value is the UK's abundance of talented, creative, innovative architects and students. Their goal and distinguishing value is their contribution to the qualities of life:

> To become an architect, 'master builder' or maître d'oeuvre it was, and still is, essential for the graduate to have studied the art and science of architecture and its fundamental principles; one who had the wisdom and spiritual insight into the nature of humanity, health and the natural world about us; one who conceived and determined the 'soul' of a building as well as controlling the total design of the setting, the exterior, the interior design, decoration and furnishing and their related

costs and buildability. An experienced qualified architect would mastermind the complete
project. As a lead consultant, the architect
understood the 'systematic arrangement of
knowledge' and devised and controlled the
grand strategy to transform a client's brief into
a project that created a building worthy of the
name of architecture.

Does this express the essence and foundation of the ARB's
training and the education required of today's architects?
Do the current cultural situations allow or even encourage
the intuitive mind to see, hear, feel and understand what
we innately sense and perceive, or have we lost (forgotten/
ignored) our innate awareness of how life and the universe
are dominated by rhythms and endlessly repeating cycles? In
March 2019, a banner headline in *The Times* read, 'Polymaths
wanted at […] Britain's first new university in 40 years'.
The article reported that top business organisations have
formed the London Interdisciplinary School to cut across
interdisciplinary boundaries to counter the narrow education
system and offer a one-degree course for 'polymaths'. The
curriculum will combine science, arts and design, technology
and the humanities to create a new style of graduate who is
more rounded and adept at solving problems.

Positive and encouraging action was also taken in
2015 when the RIBA set up the Education Review Group
representing academia and practice to analyse relevant new
models for architectural education established by schools of
architecture and other course providers. The report, intended
to be published in September 2019, will form the basis for

future RIBA validation of courses and qualifications in UK schools of architecture. In turn, this might encourage the ARB's prescriptions on the built environment to include impacts on occupants' health and well-being of mind, body and psyche; the avoidance of health hazards; and the fundamental principles of design. Such RIBA validation would embrace humanistic values in the teachings and promote the enhanced values a qualified architect brings to a project.

Work cited

Rosemary Bennett. 'Polymaths wanted at London Interdisciplinary School, Britain's first new university in 40 years', *The Times*, 1 March 2019.

CHAPTER 15

THE RIBA'S NEW CODE OF PROFESSIONAL CONDUCT

The latest RIBA Code of Conduct became effective on 1 May 2019. The Code significantly widens the scope of architects' obligations and duties:

- To the wider world
- Towards society and the end user
- Towards the commissioning services (clients may include professional clients, investors and funders)
- Towards those in the workplace (colleagues, employees, employers)
- Towards the professions
- Towards oneself.

If a conflict arises, the one that best serves the public interest takes precedence.

Further duties include:

- Ensuring a successful handover of information
- The post-occupancy evolution of the building's lifetime performance
- The impact on the natural environment

- Specialist safeguards to protect the local environment, ecology and biodiversity
- Promoting a strategy for the sustainable design, construction and operation of the built environment
- Promoting the minimisation of whole-life carbon and energy use.

This is a wake-up call for the whole profession, including the ARB's scope of the training and education curriculum. It should foster cooperation and encourage architects to take control as researchers and leaders. The after-shocks have yet to be felt.

Carys Rowlands, RIBA Head of Professional Standards, introduced the changes to the Code with this statement: 'RIBA members are the gold standard of the architectural profession – the best in the world – [and] the codes exist to ensure and protect the highest standards of professionalism [...] and members can be informed thought leaders and the go-to people in their fields of expertise.'

The introduction says the new Code has been devised to protect the reputation of RIBA members to enable them to differentiate themselves to clients and to improve the wider issues of the built environment. Significantly, the Code's radical changes refer to the architects' duties to the client, the public interest and the wider world. It now includes the architect's responsibility for addressing global issues of climate change, biodiversity and sustainable design; sustainable buildings and communities; sustainable practices, strategies, materials; the minimising of whole-life carbon energy use; the effect on community and society of conservation and ecology; and the impact on the natural environment and the safeguarding of the local environment.

According to the Code, architects: should consider; shall advise; should promote; shall advocate; shall inform and encourage; should develop; and use reasonable endeavours to persuade their clients to allow these issues to be integral to the project's brief. If a conflict of interest arises, members must either (a) remove its cause; or (b) withdraw from the situation. Presumably, RIBA members working abroad are bound by the same Code of Conduct duties, whatever a foreign country's climate change policy may be.

Already, there are many green practices that have successfully overcome the client's or project manager's reluctance to go green by highlighting the commercial benefits. Nevertheless, however ethically committed an architect may be, these global issues also need positive legislation to support the demand for urgent action.

The Code has set a course that is a major transition for the leadership role and status of the architect and the traditionally accepted architect/client relationship. As the go-to professionals, architects have a duty to lead the project teams and guide the clients instead of passively acting as a well-behaved tactical manager to produce drawings that conform to the current by-laws.

Under the Code's clause on Integrity: Members must be familiar and up to date with relevant codes of practice and guidelines that may be issued or endorsed by the Institute from time to time, especially those concerned with health and safety, ethical practice, sustainability and protection of the environment.

Undoubtedly, the new Code presents significant and major challenges to the training, education and practice of architecture. As well as the nurturing of creative design talent, the training and education needs to include the important aspects of perennial wisdom, physics *and* metaphysics – understanding the impact of the built environment on the mind, body and psyche and, in particular, how and why the function of the endocrine glands respond to the design of buildings and the built environment.

Do architects have sufficient knowledge of elementary biology to understand and deal with the hazardous effects of the built environment on the endocrine glands, which control our behaviour, health patterns and life-enhancing well-being? The pineal gland is highly sensitive to light, colour and electromagnetic fields; the pituitary gland regulates body temperature controlled by pituitary and pineal; and cortisol is the stress hormone that regulates blood pressure. The neurotransmitter secretions, serotonin and melatonin, are super-sensitive to light.

Our cells communicate by a chemical transmission of light and, according to quantum theory, everything in the universe – from living organisms to solid rocks – is composed of varying degrees of sunlight. David Staczek is a principal at ZGF architects, a practice founded on healthcare facilities. In *Architizer Journal*, July 2019, he wrote:

> Architecture, planning and design have the power to impact on our mood, affect patient outcomes in medical facilities, enhance or detract from our performance and focus […] [and] impact how we live […] Roman architect Vitruvius […] told us that buildings 'should delight people and raise their spirits'. […] Bad architecture and bad design can negatively affect us mentally and physically […] That's why we need […] good design that makes us

healthier! We must design buildings and spaces with connections to nature, balanced compositions, natural proportions and thoughtful planning that promotes a healthy lifestyle.

Do architects have an awareness of the Earth's energy fields? British researcher Serena Roney-Dougal reports on evidence that geomagnetic activity and Earth's energy fields affect the chemicals in the brain produced by the pineal gland: the enzyme involved in the production of melatonin is strongly affected by electromagnetic fields. In effect, RIBA's new Code returns full circle to Vitruvius who emphasised that it was essential for architects to have 'some knowledge of medicine'. Architects are not expected to be experts in these fields of biology and physiology, but their value would be to have the knowledge, understanding and skills to lead and deal with health and well-being.

In October 2019, RIBA announced its 2030 Climate Challenge with goals of core health and well-being targets on temperature, daylight and indoor air quality. It has set a series of targets for policies to reduce operational energy and potable water. The target for climate change is to meet zero whole-life carbon for new and retrofitted buildings.

The RIBA's new Code of Conduct, the changes to its governance and the latest Challenges are clear statements that it is not a private membership club; its purpose is to be an organisation for research, knowledge and maintaining the highest standards of training, education, leadership and practice.

Work cited

David Staczek. 'Is bad architecture harmful to our health?' *Architizer Journal*, architizer.com, 9 July 2019.

CHAPTER 16
THE CLIENTS

Ah yes, the client. We must not forget the clients – without them we have no business. The Sir Henry Wood promenade concerts are a long-standing, annual institution at the Royal Albert Hall in London and relayed throughout Britain and other parts of the world. During every performance, for the whole of the twelve-week summer season, Sir Henry Wood's bronze bust, wreathed with the fresh laurel leaves of honour, is prominently displayed in front of the organ. It faces out above the musicians, directly towards the conductor and the audience. The bust is a simple symbol of acknowledgement and gratitude to Sir Henry for his dedication to building the repertoire and institution of the Proms.

This is how clients and customers should be regarded, acknowledged and blessed for keeping us in business. Their best interests should be embedded in the structure and culture of our own organisations. By the same token, clients and customers should remember that the successful promenade concerts have thrived and survived over the years because Sir Henry and all his appointed successors have properly planned the programmes and performances and set the ticket-pricing at acceptable levels. This is just a kindly reminder for commercial clients and contractors that the abolition of the RIBA scale of charges in 1982 was an unnecessary act of self-harm.

The vote to abandon the well-established scale of fees decision has had far-reaching and unintended consequences that have reduced a practice's income. Current guidelines have produced a fee-bidding process that can be exploited by penny-pinching clients who are free to negotiate the fees, basing the appointment on price rather than expertise, quality of service and end-product value. Often, the financial rewards are not commensurate with the extent and value of the architect's input.

Parallel with the increasing complexities of planning laws and building code regulations, as well as the demand for high-performance technology, there has been the tendency on the part of clients, and the public at large, to become more litigious. This is yet another unavoidable distraction that engages the architects' attention towards protecting themselves from claims of negligence rather than expending energy on the core fundamental principles of architecture. The seemingly ever-increasing regulations imposed by the government and European Union have added to architects' workload and decreased their fee earnings and profitability.

The 958 participants in the RIBA Client Survey 2016 equally represented private domestic clients, contractors and commercial clients. Architects acting for private domestic clients received the highest scores for design and meeting the brief. Contractors gave them the lowest score, while commercial clients rated architects' skills in management, commercial understanding, programming and adding value as less than satisfactory. (Not much change there then since the 1963 changes to the Part 3 curriculum.)

The results suggest that when a client selects the appointment of an architect through personal recommendation or repeat works, there is greater trust and rapport. Whereas, and particularly in the case of commercial clients, when the architect's appointment has been based on price competition – often instigated by the project manager – the outcome can be affected. No doubt, members provide the RIBA Client Liaison Group with ample information, rating the working practices and cooperation of their clients and contractors that would generally improve any current lack of trust. Architects need the opportunity to comment on fair and adequate fees, realistic programming, procurement practices and the most beneficial role for project management that can have profound impacts on their contribution and value.

The most valued opinions on the performance of architects and their contribution to a project will come from a client. Good listening will establish the qualities and expertise a client needs from the architect and what the architect needs from a client. It improves relationships when architects do not assume that their client 'sees' the drawings and screen images as well as they do. Some clients are indeed visually orientated; others may be auditorily orientated and would prefer to be talked through the scheme; others may be kinaesthetically orientated and would prefer to touch and feel a drawing or model.

Conformance to legislation continues to be the main driving force requiring architects to design solely in accordance with the client's commercial requirements and their property agent advisers. However, the RIBA's new Code of Conduct, which came into force in May 2019, means that members can no longer solely satisfy the demands of their clients. The new

Code also imposes a duty towards the general public and the wider world. This could yet turn out to be a major turning point in professional relationships. The Code also reinforces the need for architects to be innovators and initiators and not wait for the likes of Sir Edwin Chadwick and Florence Nightingale to campaign to achieve government legislation.

Architects now have an obligation and professional duty to address biodiversity, climate change, sustainable development, ecology and building performance and social changes to create healthy and life-enhancing environments affecting the way we live our lives. They must also encourage and persuade clients to go green.

These changes will have a significant impact on the architect's role, remit, relevance and value as leaders who set social, political and cultural agendas. It will demand significant changes to the way architects are trained, educated and practice, and radically reinforces the duties required of architects and their clients to create a built environment.

We have now come full circle to emulate the ethos of the earlier master sages and architects who practised architecture to protect and enhance the health and well-being of their fellow citizens. This is also, more or less, a repeat pattern of the circumstances since the treatise on clientship was written by Vitruvius more than 2,000 years ago. The onus is also on the patron and client, who commissions the buildings, and not on the architect alone, to be well informed about architecture, which has the power to enhance and enrich the life of the citizens. In other words: good architecture = a good architect + a good client.

According to the 5,000-year-old Hindu tradition, the souls of both the architect and the donor (the client) were inseparably involved in the success of a building's final form. That form had to be sufficiently geometrically accurate (sacred) for the gods to be compelled to be present. Whether a private dwelling or a commercial or public building, the architect alone cannot produce a sacred vehicle for the expression of a 'spiritual presence and a space for the heart' without the client and users of the building understanding and sharing that same vision. Whenever we approach and enter a building designed according to the universal laws or canon, all the vibrations created by the Earth's energy fields, the geometry, the colour and sound will resonate with the whole of our being. Subliminally, our senses and every part of our body will see, hear and feel these vibrations and at the most subtle level, our psyche will respond to the occult wave patterns. Physically, biologically, intellectually, emotionally, spiritually and joyfully, we will be reminded of our common bond with nature. We will feel healed and the building, whether it be humble or grand, will be a temple of the soul.

Members of the RIBA have always had a duty to honour and uphold its motto to be of service for the citizens and the glory of the city. Now, under the new Code, architects must also be of service for the planet.

PART III

THOUGHTS ON
THE ARCHITECT IN PRACTICE

CHAPTER 17
The Role of the Architect

As ever, the profession of architecture is well endowed with an abundance of highly talented and dedicated students and practitioners. Its core principles are based on metaphysics that deal with abstract concepts, the nature of being and the investigation into objects and their properties, space and time, cause and effect, aesthetics, concepts, values, viewpoints, physiology, biology and the human psyche. These principles are the foundation of an architect's status and value to society.

The role of a twentieth-century qualified architect was based on a minimum of seven years' conventional training and education:

- To design the orientation, siting, landscape, the overall volume, shape, size and external appearance of the building
- To be in direct contact with the client and propose the required members of the team according to the type and content of a particular project
- To act as the project's strategist and leader of the team
- To control building estimates and budgets
- To inspect and control the programme and construction of the work on site
- To approve interim and final accounts.

Do architects have a knowledge and understanding of the holistic nature of human beings and the natural world, and the skills to deal with both the beneficial and adverse effects that the siting, design and construction of any building will have on the health, well-being and psyche of the occupants? Has the curriculum changed and evolved to keep pace with the global issues of the twenty-first century? Have architects been trained to become leaders and innovators or to act as obedient managers and followers? The prevailing compartmentalised role has trended away from leadership towards management and conformance with regulations and legislation. Despite advanced technology and the mass of available data, if compliance is the paramount requirement, why are many new towns, estates and buildings bad for our health, soulless and often a source of personal sickness and social dysfunction?

Architecture is about creating life-enhancing urban environments and spaces for people to live in, work in, play in, learn in and be healed inside buildings where we now spend the vast majority of our lives. The layout, volumes, proportions and design features of interior spaces should be one of the architect's main focuses of attention and yet views of interior spaces are often played down or omitted when architects present their designs for a new project. Often, a design presentation is only the plans, sections and external elevations, which might be accompanied by a model or artist's impression to illustrate the massing and materials of the façade. (An architect's plans and sections will indicate the measure of their interest and understanding of interior design.) How can the exterior of a building be detached from what goes on inside? In the same manner, our facial expressions, body language, words and deeds are external reflections of our psycho/spiritual inner being.

The quality of the interior environment, the colours, light and shade, proportions, volumes, the siting and swing of doors, the placing of interior features and furniture and so on, and how the building will be used and by whom are integral aspects to every building design concept. It is not surprising that the vacuum left by architects has been filled by professional interior design specialists. To a large extent, they have become far more prominent and important than the architect, because they have taken control of the interior elements that have greater impact on our day-to-day lives. (Interior design specialists are not to be confused with interior decorators, sometimes disparagingly called 'inferior decorators'.)

The role of the architect, and the teaching and practice of architecture, has been in a state of transition for decades. Treating interior design as a separate discipline is just one of the several spheres of work and services that has contributed to the fragmentation of the profession of architecture and allowed others to take over.

The growth in the demand for taller, larger, high-performance buildings and the construction industry's development of equipment and the furnishing of buildings using non-traditional materials, new machines and building techniques, has tended to lead to the use of many new, untried, untested products and systems without a comprehensive evaluation of the impact on the ecology, sustainability and the health and well-being of the construction operatives and those who occupy the completed building. It has also created a breed of specialists and experts with specialised disciplines to add to the project team.

These advancements in building technology and systems have demanded the collaboration and input of skilled specialists who make significant contributions to a project within their field of operation. A project's professional team can often include architects, quantity surveyors, structural and mechanical engineers, health and safety advisers, toxic materials specialists, IT and computer experts, building control and environmental and ecology specialists as well as acoustic engineers, lighting designers, landscape architects, crime prevention advisers, robotic construction managers, et al.

Their training follows the tenets of modern science. It deals in physics and mechanics and calculates the world. A quantity surveyor calculates and measures the cost of painting and the quantity of paint; only the architect has, or should have, the knowledge to evaluate the effect a chosen colour has on our mind, body and psyche. For example, painting a hospital mental health ward yellow would impact on the endocrine glands and create higher stress levels for the patients.

Specialised demarcation has changed the conventional role of the architect. Control of the building estimates and budgets is now the sole responsibility of the cost control manager or quantity surveyor; control of the complete programme and construction is now undertaken by the project manager or the project construction manager who controls the works on site. Now, the leader and team selector is the ubiquitous project manager through whom all of the team's procurement contracts and communications are passed. Everyone in the team is needed to give tactical support to each other, but only the architect has, or should have been, trained to mastermind the grand strategy that transforms a building design worthy of the name of architecture.

Why has the whole profession – its members, the institutions and the schools – allowed the architect's role as *maître d'oeuvre* to be eroded and their position and status relinquished as the project leader? Fragmentation has encouraged clients and project managers to engage architects to 'draw up plans' to create a wind and watertight envelope to house all the requirements designed and specified by others. This has demoted the architect's role and status to a cameo bit-part designing attractive façades much like a make-up artist or theatrical costumier produces whatever period and dramatic effect may be desired. (A form of *façadism* is how it works in the automobile industry: the 'designers' deal with all the engineering, mechanical parts, construction and production of a car – otherwise known in the building industry as 'the professional team'. The outer appearance, colour combinations and the latest trendy external features and look of the car is created by a stylist).

The significant number of major new UK building projects procured under a 'design and build' or Private Finance Initiative (PFI) contract has further highlighted the trend to erode the role of architects. The professional team, including the architect, is appointed by the main contractor who acts as the 'client' with total and direct control over the whole design, specification and construction of the building. Often, the architect is not even allowed to have any direct contact with the building owner or developer. Might budget pruning explain why certain PFI schools and hospitals have obscure, unwelcoming main entrances that are difficult to locate?

Are architects appointed for their strategic leadership skills or are they retained as tame, well-behaved subservient tacticians to 'do the drawings', to design façades to create whatever dramatic effect the client or planning officer may approve? Clients and project managers should bear in mind that no one in the project's professional team can operate and take action until the architect draws a line. It is 'the stuff that dreams are made on' for all those who yearn for a return to Rudofsky's architecture without architects – a Utopian world where no one is needed even to 'do the drawings'.

Already there are changes in the air. Architects are adapting to prefabrication and a move towards a collaborative design process with manufacturers as well as using alternative forms of procurement. Some are carrying out their own developments while others have set up their own academies, and specialist 'boutiques' are being established to offer unique design services and expertise.

Another trend is the healthy scepticism of academic theorists. Students and graduates are turning to commercially experienced polymath lecturers such as the internationally respected Derek Clements-Croome, Professor Emeritus Reading University. His extensive works on the beneficial impact that the design of healthy and sustainable, intelligent buildings have on their occupants' health, behaviour, comfort, well-being and psyche address the issues of sustainability, ecologically viable and sensory design, climate change and the prudent avoidance of harmful electromagnetic fields and subterranean energy fields.

Aspects of the architects' role have been marginalised by the specialised technical expertise of other members of a professional team, but this has created positive opportunities and advantages that can allow architects to focus more on the essence and fundamental principles of architecture.

Suggested further reading

D. J. Clements-Croome, ed. 'Effects of the Built Environment on Health and Wellbeing' in *Creating the productive workplace: places to work creatively*, Routledge, London, 2018.

D.J. Clements-Croome, ed. 'Sustainable Healthy Intelligent Buildings for People' in *Intelligent Buildings*, ICE, 2013.

CHAPTER 18
THE ARCHITECT IN PRACTICE

The practice of architecture has always been subjected to the vagaries of clients, politics, economics, business ethics and controls, inventions, new materials, cultural fashions, regulations, crises and natural events. While the practical day-to-day business of building and running a practice is about budgets, fees, legalities, materials, construction, techniques and functional space, there is an intrinsic, perennial core role of the architect that remains as constant today as it has throughout history. The essence of that core is leadership and innovation based upon the natural laws of the universe and serving the health, well-being and spirit of the people and the built environment. Few Western schools of architecture teach humanistic philosophy.

During the early post-war period many clients and contractors felt their architects had been notoriously weak on matters of business management. There was poor financial constraint; unpunctual delivery of drawings and information; lax practical engineering; slack on-site inspection and supervision; the indulgent use of the latest, untested material or construction technique; and often vague indifference to the function and design of the interiors of the building. Dissatisfied clients also complained that architects were too compliant with the demands imposed by town planning officers and other bureaucrats.

Of course, not all architects can be accused of possessing some or any of these negative qualities, but perhaps it has been forever thus, since people first engaged the services of a professional to advise them on designing a building for their own requirements. According to Vitruvius in Book VI of *The Ten Books on Architecture*:

> Hence it was that the ancients used to entrust their work in the first place to architects [who] had been properly educated [...] But when I see that this grand art is boldly professed by the uneducated and the unskilful, and by men who, far from being acquainted with architecture, have no knowledge even of the carpenter's trade, I can find nothing but praise for those householders who, in the confidence of learning, are emboldened to build for themselves. Their judgement is that, if they must trust to inexperienced persons, it is more becoming to them to use up a good round sum at their own pleasure than that of a stranger.

The RIBA Council recognised that urgent action was needed to address their valid criticisms. It acknowledged that, generally, architects were not well gifted in office management, administration, accounting, keeping time and fee records, marketing, PR, bottom-line accounting and dealing with myriad laws and regulations. In response, the RIBA launched a bold and unique training programme for the postgraduate Part 3 Professional Practice examinations. It included contract administration and business management to encourage architects to become as proficient as their clients, contractors and other members of a project team.

More than fifty-five years on from the 1963 launch, the RIBA bookshop has an abundance of practice manuals and tool boxes, guides on corporate responsibilities and office practice, and shelves of books on business and project management systems, but there is very little on actual leadership. No doubt there has been a marked improvement in practice administration, but the pendulum began to swing to the other extreme, and the business of efficiently running a practice may have tended to become more important than the architect's core role.

At the same time, a worldwide social, economic and business revolution based on the transmission of information, computerisation, communication and advances in technology began to transform traditional pre-war practices. This rapid advancement in technology has affected every aspect of daily life. According to Dr Jeremy Naydler's book, we now live our lives *In the Shadow of the Machine*. We calculate the world instead of understanding it. Computer-aided design (CAD) had a significant impact in architects' offices. Drawing boards propped up on a couple of house bricks disappeared almost overnight and suddenly everyone was staring at CAD screens. A steady stream of new technical advances revolutionised the production and issue of drawings and the systems of internal and external communications. Elimination of the typing pools and secretarial staff have also led to careless drafting of instructions and paper trail vulnerabilities.

While demarcation, marginalisation and undervaluation continue to be the profession's high-priority concerns and topics of debate, architects appear to be in thrall to the ever-developing advances in technology. Since the digital age of information technology that began in the 1970s, technology has become the new global opiate that dominates every aspect of life and living. The need to be abreast of the latest materials and electronic devices may tend to overburden and preoccupy architects' practices at the expense of a project's essential values and the design concept.

Information has tended to repudiate, diminish or even extinguish the essential values of knowledge, imagination, creativity, wisdom, skills and leadership that were the foundation of the training, education and practice of the master architects. Information is not a synonym for knowledge and understanding. Information is bare facts; knowledge is skills and mastery acquired through experience, training and education. Understanding is perception and intelligent behaviour in the application of knowledge. As Albert Einstein observed, 'Any fool can know. The point is to understand.'

Information technologies are tools for processing data. The ancient Chinese invention of paper was a tool that aided the creativity of writers and artists. Computers are tools for aiding drawing – they are not the designers. A Kalashnikov rifle is a tool for killing people – it is not the killer. (An old Celtic proverb tells us: Never give a sword to a man who can't dance.)

Tools are invaluable for those who have had the training, education and experience to know what information they need and understand why they need it. We now depend on computers to store and retrieve information – they conveniently save us the trouble of *remembering*. Are we in danger of losing the facility to use our brains to retrieve facts that may be useful to apply to other future situations?

Artificial Intelligence (AI) is a virtual world connected to the natural world about us but devoid of human sensuality and sensory experiences of touch, smell, heat and cold, wind and rain. This virtual world is produced by a machine to mimic natural human intelligence in making decisions. It produces statements or predictions using data based on the mathematics of probabilities originally expounded by the ancient Greek Euclid. Computer programmers, using computer system algorithms, write software that produces possible outcomes predicted on their expert knowledge and experiential evidence to carry out tasks in human ways.

AI is prediction based on the mathematics of probabilities; the predictions are not certainties and depend on the qualities and skills of the programmers' expert knowledge of human psychology, neuron networks, mathematics, biology and computer science. The danger is to treat AI as *reality* without due scepticism and innate, intuitive discernment. Software engineers are clever people who are good at training machines to mimic human behaviour and output. Their motives and purpose may not always be in the best interests of people, ecology, sustainability and the planet. AI is built on resonance and can trick people into exposing their preferences – toffee or chocolate? – and then design algorithms that allow advertising to target them accordingly.

Building Information Modelling (BIM) was conceived in the 1970s. Twenty years later, the software was commercially available and is now the next leap forward in management tools. BIM is a digital resource of information on the design and function of a building that can be shared with all of a project's stakeholders in order to aid decisions during the whole-life cycle from concept to maintenance and ultimate demolition. It is not endowed with knowledge, understanding and skills; BIM is a *tool* to provide *information*. To work effectively it needs the cooperation and collaboration of all the stakeholders and all the information to be fully coordinated by working to a selected coordinated 'key' that generates the entire architectural design, services and installation. Nothing new there then – this is how medieval healer-priests and Palladio through to the 2003 RIBA Gold Medallist Rafael Moneo used the perennial teachings of Plato, Vitruvius, and all the great architects, to design their buildings.

BIM software has evolved through several incarnations that have changed the way buildings are designed, procured, managed and occupied, and how information is communicated. Provided they have the knowledge, understanding and skills in these subjects, BIM can aid architects to address a design's impact on sustainability, ecology, biodiversity, climate change, health and well-being. And provided also that the software writers know what they are writing about and continue to keep abreast of developments on these subjects. (Again: Never give a man a sword until he knows how to dance).

BIM will shake up the professional businesses of cost management, project management, construction management, facility management, modular coordination and prefabrication. The other good news is that the use of BIM and the latest RIBA Code of Conduct will demand radical changes to the training, education and practice of architecture and return architects to being the go-to people for leadership and innovation and know-how. It might also encourage clients to trust the opinions of their architects rather than the project managers.

The tools of AI are integral to the design and construction of the built environment. It is essential that architects have sufficient knowledge and understanding of human behaviour, psychology and biology to avoid an unquestioning faith in the predictions based on the opinions and interpretations of these anonymous AI programmers. The world has become a global village and whether we are Western city dwellers or Amazonian Indians living in the depths of the jungle, our life and the way we live will be affected, to a lesser or far greater extent, by the all-pervading information technologies and the global external forces of international property development, commerce and politics.

The latest RIBA Plan of Work 2013, revised in 2017, sets out the architect's roles as: Project Leader, Lead Designer, Architect, Contract Administrator, Lead Consultant, Project Co-ordinator, Interior Designer.

Leadership is a talent and a gift; management is a reliable servant. If everyone in the team, including the architect, is a tactical manager, who is supposed to be a project's grand strategist and leader? With due respect to the fourteen authors who contributed to the RIBA document, aren't these classifications more likely to perpetuate the fragmentation and undermining of the architect's role as a project's strategic leader and senior consultant, otherwise known simply as the architect? Should architects have to decide which hat to wear for any given appointment, or endure the confusion, in the words of the vernacular, of not knowing whether they are punched, bored or countersunk?

There is an urgent task for the whole profession to investigate what has caused the negative fragmentation of the role of the architect. Until the distinguished and distinguishing values are progressed and established, it is unlikely that clients, project managers and the general public will understand and appreciate the comprehensive service and value of the architect's work.

Since 2015, the RIBA has been reviewing the training and education of architects – addressed in the new 2019 Code of Conduct – together with other initiatives. The task of restoring members' confidence, status and role is being guided by Sir Nicholas Grimshaw's current series of seminars on leadership. Does this suggest that the current ARB curriculum does not adequately provide the training and education to equip the graduate architects with the necessary knowledge, understanding and skills of organisation and leadership?

Work cited

Jeremy Naydler. *In the Shadow of the Machine*, Temple Lodge Press, 2018.

Suggested further reading

Thomas Saunders. *Getting A Life*, SilverWood Books, 2014. (The Thomas Saunders Partnership pp 75–134).

CHAPTER 19

LEADERSHIP AND MANAGEMENT

Strategy and Tactics

The Owl and the Worm

A worm, making its way along the forest floor, stops at a huge log. It tries to crawl over but falls back. It keeps trying until it lies exhausted and gasping for breath.

An owl (a wise bird) calls to the worm:

You will never crawl over that log.

I know, but what can I do?

The only way is to fly over.

OK, so how do I get wings?

I can't answer that question. I only deal in broad strategic principles.

There is strategy *and* tactics. They are not synonymous.

Leadership is strategy. Management is tactics

Most acutely in wartime, understanding the difference between strategy and tactics is a matter of winning and losing, life and death. The goal or target of the Allies in World War 2 was to win the war. It was decided that could only be achieved by defeating Germany on its own soil. The commanders-in-chief had a number of strategic options for attacking the shores of Europe – either through Norway, or the Balkans, or Italy, or through France via Calais or Cherbourg.

While the Allied command settled on Cherbourg, there were a few generals, as ever, who thought it would be a good idea to simultaneously attack other targets such as the Dardanelles or Holland. Had the Allied command not resisted these sideshow operations, it would have dissipated the strategic effort and reduced the overall concentration of forces and materiel with disastrous consequences. It was the Allied command's strategic role to decide what to do, when to do it and to provide the necessary resources to carry out the task. (The word *decide* springs from the same origins as infanticide and suicide, meaning *to kill*. So, when you stop prevaricating and finally decide what to do, it kills off the various options and allows you to focus all your effort and energies on taking action. Bear in mind the warning of Prussian field marshal Helmuth Von Moltke: 'No plan survives the first contact with the enemy.') The role of the Allied command tacticians – from the field generals to the sergeant majors – was to establish procedures to organise and control the use of available resources and to manage the training and feeding of the troops to execute the planned strategy. There is no such thing as *grand* tactics, but rank and file managers also need leadership qualities to carry out the strategy.

Leadership

According to lauded management expert Peter Drucker, 'Only three things happen naturally in organisations: friction, confusion and underperformance. Everything else requires leadership.' There is leadership *and* management. They are not synonymous.

The qualities of leadership:
- Doing the right things
- Striving to be of service to others rather than oneself
- Being free of the tyranny of sales and bottom line targets
- Striving for excellence – not perfection
- Balancing virtue and economy to create harmony
- Making decisions on the spot at the proper time, without prevarication or wavering and acceptance of full responsibility for the outcome
- Without fear of the unknown, not striving for certainty
- Accepting that analysis of the past is not a guide for the future
- Envisaging the next five years
- Fostering talent and encouraging personal development and a work-life balance
- Striving for something greater than oneself
- Acting with clarity, incisiveness, and depending on intuitive feelings

Leadership is being a good listener and learner. People need their voice to be heard. Listen intently to what is *not* being said. According to Warrant Officer Glen Haughton, the British army's most senior sergeant major, 'Soldiers want to be heard and they want to feel valued. They have a huge amount to offer and we as an army could draw a huge amount from them if we give them a voice.'

If a leader wants to know about the organisation's problems, don't ask management, simply allow and encourage the staff to speak freely. Bear in mind Plato's dictum: Everyone is innately gifted with knowledge and wisdom. All we can do is find the teachers who will help us to remember.

Leadership is not about authoritarian control but motivating and guiding good action, management and *followship*. Honesty and integrity are essential qualities as well as having the vision to set targets or goals and the skills to communicate with managers and the general staff to influence and inspire everyone with the same desire to carry out the work towards a strategic goal. With radical, caring candour, the talent is not to direct but to guide, inform and create an environment and culture that encourages people to grow, develop, improve and feel they are at the heart of things, which gives their work meaning.

'The deepest drive in the human spirit is to be acknowledged' observed Stephen R. Covey, author of *The 7 Habits of Highly Effective People*.

A good leader focuses on the right action and the right timing – not the outcome. It is posing the right question and taking action when things go wrong. In Homer's *Odyssey*, Odysseus, the captain of the ship, had to take strong action to haul his sailors back on board before the crew were seduced into a drugged stupor of forgetfulness (unconsciousness) and lethargy by the Lotus Eaters. Otherwise, he would never be able return home to Ithaca.

No Water, no Moon (Zen koan)

When the nun Chiyono studied Zen she was unable to attain the fruits of meditation for a long time. At last one moonlit night she was carrying water in an old pail bound with bamboo. The bamboo broke and the bottom fell out of the pail, and at that moment Chiyono was set free. She wrote in a poem:

> In this way and that, I tried to save the old pail
> Since the bamboo strip was weakening and about to break
> Until at last the bottom fell out
> No more water in the pail!
> No more moon in the water!

She had looked up, and seeing the unreflected Moon realised that the moon in the water and the moon in the sky are not the same thing, and became enlightened. (The Buddha said, 'All beings are born enlightened, but it takes a lifetime to discover this.') If we are always looking down, we only see the reflections of our self-consciousness and emotions. When we aspire to wisdom and look up, we can experience Plato's *truth, beauty and goodness*.

Charles Handy, doyen of business management, cites archetypal characters in Greek mythology in his book *Gods of Management* to illustrate styles of organisational cultures and leadership. Zeus leaders are the traditional taskmaster boss; Apollo leaders are bureaucratic and resist change; and Athena leaders create diverse team cultures. Dionysus leaders are gifted individualists who are best at working as a sole-trader; 'organisation' is anathema to Dionysian types.

In Chapter 24 of this book we will meet other mythical gods and fairy tales.

Management

There is management *and* managerialism. They are not synonymous. To quote Peter Drucker again: 'Most of what we call management consists of making it difficult for people to get on with their work.'

Business management

Business management is a generic term that includes: management of managers; management of finance; management of accounting and administration office systems; management of human resources; management of materials; management of projects; management of marketing; management of sales; management of IT; management of allied professionals; management of clients, and so on.

The Business Dictionary's definition of management:

Management consists of the interlocking functions of creating corporate policy, and organising, planning, controlling and directing an organisation's resources in order to activate the objectives of that policy.

Qualities of managers and management:

- A manager's first job is to manage
- Making possible the goal
- Resisting over-ruling and interference
- Encouraging the manager's team to contribute to the management

Marketing decisions should be left to marketing managers to focus on the business of marketing. It is not the manager's job to maximise profit but to provide sufficient profit to cover the risk of economic activity. The problem (or state of chaos) occurs when managers provide the right answer to the strategic leader's wrong question.

'Proper management always results in sustainable and profitable growth.' (Jérôme Chouchan, *Target: Business Wisdom from the Ancient Japanese Martial Art of Kyudo*)

Managerialism

Managerialism can be defined as a myth. A myth is a traditional story typically involving supernatural beings or events or a widely held but false belief. In his book *Managerialism* Thomas Klikauer offers this description:

> Managerialism combines management of knowledge and ideology to establish itself systematically in organisations and society while depriving owners, employees (organisational-economical) and civil society (social-political) of all decision-making powers. Managerialism justifies the application of managerial techniques to all areas of society on the grounds of superior ideology, expert training, and the exclusive possession of managerial knowledge necessary to efficiently run corporations and societies.

Management + ideology + expansion of power = Managerialism
Managerialism abandons democracy and social harmony. It ignores the needs, desires, work satisfaction, cultural values and the positive motivation of human beings. It is a pernicious dogma based on neo-Marxism. Managerialism

is a subversive, hierarchical, elitist, authoritarian dominance often run by self-appointed or unelected individuals or groups.

Managerialism, disguised as Management, includes:

Management of conformance; management of gender pay gap; management of gender fluidity; management of political correctness; management of Human Resources (HR); management of free speech, management of the European Union's General Data Protection Regulations (GDPR) and so on.

Universal red-tape strangulation

This is a story adapted from Sir John Timpson's weekly column, 'Straight-talking, common sense from the front line of management' in the business section of *The Daily Telegraph*, 4 June 2018:

> Once upon a time in the sixties, an office was full of clerks using adding machines and Kardex records to analyse stock and sales [until] a salesman promised that his new computer would replace the old-fashioned systems within three years. It took two decades before the clerks and machines had gone, only to be replaced by more expensive managers and staff of compliance to tick every box of all the legal requirements of government and the European Parliament regulations. These ever-expanding monitoring departments make little or no contribution to creating

its commercial success and main aims of a business. These managers are paid some of the highest salaries in business.

Eventually, the business is overwhelmed and its life-blood is sucked out by the do-gooders who are obsessed with setting rules and regulations until the organisation dies of red-tape strangulation. Is this the way the NHS, social services, universities and governments are run?

The Ghost of Stasi

Once upon a time – 1949 to be precise – the German Democratic Republic of East Germany created its tyrannical State Security Service called Stasi whose sole task was to spy on their own population. Eventually, all the staff dispersed and disappeared in 1990. Then, the European Union's covert wizards of Brussels waved their magic wands and the Stasi was reincarnated as the obscure, sinister managerialism departments that expand and infiltrate business organisations and the whole of society. It is a pernicious, global, secret movement motivated to achieve political ends that has nothing or little to do with economics and prosperity. There is a growing army of captains of industry, entrepreneurs and other political revolutionaries who are beginning to clear out these subversives and their punitive regulations.

Sadly, this story is neither a myth nor a fairy tale. (The ex-Stasi could become rehabilitated and continue their life's purpose in the UK's secret services MI5 and MI6, which is currently advertising a recruitment drive.)

Client entertainment

Sadly, this is another story that is neither a myth nor fairy tale:

> Once upon a time – 2018 to be precise – the CEO of a bank in the City of London invited a couple of his existing clients to a corporate event. The clients' Compliance Department's rules demanded that all invitations must be reported and approved. Not unusually, the application to accept the invitation was rejected. No reason was offered by the Compliance manager. Disagreement or rational dialogue are rarely permitted. It is now customary, when a business invites a client for lunch, that the client must ask how much the lunch has cost as he/she must report it to their Compliance Department.

Before these views are criticised as paranoia, please read George Orwell's prophetic book *1984* in which Great Britain is a province called Airstrip One. The global, one-party super state Oceania is governed by Big Brother – an unknown, non-existing entity with absolute power to serve its own political ends. It has no interest in people, their opinions and well-being, welfare, cultural values and traditions. Rebellion is urgently needed to exercise innate common sense and sense of values to eradicate and cleanse the pandemic virus of managerialism.

Works cited

Stephen R Covey. *The 7 Habits of Highly Effective People*, Free Press, 1989.

Jérôme Chouchan, *Target: Business Wisdom from the Ancient Japanese Martial Art of Kyudo*, LID Publishing, 2018.

Thomas Klikauer. *Managerialism,* Pelgrave MacMillan, 2013.

George Orwell. *1984,* Penguin Books, London, 1989.

Charles Handy. *Gods of Management,* Souvenir Press, 1988.

CHAPTER 20
ORGANISATION STRUCTURES

An organisation's purpose

The purpose of a business organisation is to create clients and customers. Without a client or customer, there is no business to organise. The success of a business can depend on how well it understands the client and customer and their organisation structures. They are also the best teachers to reveal your own organisation's strengths and weaknesses. (According to Peter Drucker, 'The Customer [Client] rarely buys what the company is selling.')

Whether the organisation is a vast international conglomerate, a professional practice or a sole-trader business, it will need to be led and managed by the organisation's command and control (C&C) – the chairperson, the CEO and board directors, the partners in partnership. Mum and Dad running the corner shop is no exception. If you are an employee, an employer of a large practice, or a self-employed owner, or the CEO of Marks & Spencer, the President of the RIBA or the NHS, or a flight sergeant or the air vice-marshal, or a clerk, or the leader of Haringey Council, or the prime minister, or a member of the Royal Family – *You are there to serve and to be of service.* (During the chaotic struggles for control in the House of Commons during the late summer of 2019, a member of Parliament would get full marks for honestly expressing his blatant ambition for power, when he said, 'I would love to be the prime minister.' Where, if at all, would 'To be of service to the citizens and the realm' feature in his priorities and list of duties?)

An organisation's ideal goal is to achieve the successful leadership and management of the organisation to produce economic results to make a profit in order to stay in business in order to continue to serve clients, customers, employees and society. The goal should not be profit, sales, bottom lines, maximising the wealth of owners, shareholders, directors and partners, or gaining political power. The goal is to be of service and provide satisfaction to the client, customer, the workforce, the community and the environment. This is now enshrined in the 2006 Companies Act.

It is the strategy, personal characteristics, temperament and style of communication of the leaders and managers that determines the business culture, success and staff morale. Ideally, the lines of management control should not exceed seven people.

A sign of an organisation's growth and development is when it must keep moving from one location to a number of larger premises. There is a popularly held view that as soon as it finally builds its own grand headquarters, it can retard expansion and fall into a sluggish, downhill decline.

The structure

The purpose of a structure plan is to indicate to everyone inside the organisation, and to the outside world, how the organisation operates with lines of responsibilities and who reports to whom. Ideally, the form of structure produces an efficient, caring, flexible and innovative environment where the organisation and its staff can develop and thrive. The workforce is its greatest asset and lifeblood. The smaller the distance between employers and employees, the greater the job satisfaction and commitment, the higher the quality of work and the lower the absenteeism and staff turnover.

As the business expands, there will be a tendency for the organisation's structure to develop variations of a prototype pyramid, submarine or lotus plant.

A pyramid structure

The Great Pyramid of Giza is an ancient monolithic structure. It was built by thousands of slaves as a tomb or as a building for mystical initiations – or whatever? Its purpose remains a mystery. The exterior was a polished white limestone façade covering the dense mass of rough-cut blocks of boulders. The top-most apex slabs are the only remnants of its once shining edifice and what we see today is the rough, crumbling rubble. There are just two vents: they are so dark and narrow that stars can be seen at any time of day.

In the depths of the monument are the two, so-called, King's and Queen's chambers. To get to the King's chamber you have to crawl on your hands and knees to climb the long, hot, sweaty Grand Gallery. You have to stoop to enter the small oppressive enclosure with a granite sarcophagus that is so large it must have been installed as they were building the chamber. Napoleon told his lieutenants to wait outside while he went inside the chamber. Later, it was reported that while standing alone in the chamber, he had strange hallucinations. (What else need be said?)

In a pyramid structure in a modern business organisation, the command and control executive offices are located in the polished white marble apex. A shallow pyramid can work well for small organisations where the leader and managers are in close contact and directly accessible to the staff, but as the business develops, the pyramid is jacked up to accommodate the increasing workforce and the strategic command offices become more remote from the tactical activities, which tends to foster wasteful bureaucracy and hierarchical control. In turn, this can lead to an inward, implosive vision that is designed to meet internal targets and bottom lines. The staff gets 'buried' further down in the depths of obfuscation, and the lack of delegation and inflexibility breeds a culture of *this is how we have always done it*. When the prime target of the organisation becomes its own internal operations, it can obscure and downgrade the best interests of its clients, customers, staff and the outside world. *No Water, no Moon.*

A submarine structure

A submarine is a streamlined, underwater craft that can remain below the surface for long periods. The command and control conning tower or bridge is heavily reinforced, but the main hull of the boat is only lightly protected. The only view of the outside world is through a periscope that gives a myopic, restricted field of vision to the sole operator – the captain. The crew, incarcerated in the claustrophobic conditions of the hull, are 'blinded' with no means to see the outside environment or even know where they are and in what direction the boat is heading. Neither can they have any idea about the location of a specific target.

When the captain sees a particular target through the periscope, it is only the captain who decides on the position, range and angle, when to take aim and when to shoot. If the aim fails to score a direct hit or 'kill', the tendency may be to blame the officers and crew. The effectiveness of a submarine depends on secrecy and hiding undetected until the moment to strike the elusive target.

The command and control of a submarine organisation is entirely in the hands of an omnipotent leader who is reluctant to delegate or share his or her authority. When absent or temporarily incapacitated, the leader does not hand over control to an appointed deputy to use their own initiative. Instead, all the managers are expected get in a huddle and try to second-guess what the leader would do in such circumstances. At the same time, the workforce must continue to act obediently, never question or offer a viewpoint and do what they were hired to do, until they leave the job as soon as possible or die of boredom and neglect.

When the sole, creative entrepreneur is the command and control, with a small, devoted workforce, the submarine form of organisation can be ultra-efficient and successful. Submarine structures can also work where there is the more traditionally Eastern type of culture based on disciplined deference towards the elders of the family, the captains of a boat or plane or the CEO of a business. Things can go seriously awry when the captain takes the wrong course and the co-pilot is either reluctant, or refuses, to take action to correct the obvious error.

A lotus structure

Lotus plants are a Buddhist and Hindu symbol of enlightenment, purity of body, speech and mind, and fertility. They represent openness and organic growth. The flowers and leaves float on the surface of water with their roots firmly bedded in the common source of the Earth's fertile nutrients below. To be accurate, an aquatic plant with flowers and leaves floating on the surface is a water lily of the perennial genus *Nymphaea* genus. The lotus genus *Nelumbo* may look the same, but the flowers and leaves are emergent – they rise above the water level. It is a different species and can be confused with the lotus-eaters in Homer's *Odyssey* who were eating *Nymphaea stellata* – a narcotic, psychotropic water lily that induces sleep, forgetfulness and apathy.

In a lotus structure, the command and control of the organisation is located in the central, open flower. The managed departments are the leaves with a direct access to the flower and the other surrounding satellite department leaves. Each leaf can develop and independently grow without reducing the direct and immediate connection with the control centre and the other satellite managers and staff. The whole organism can organically expand and evolve at varying speeds and volume without disturbing the life of the plant, provided it follows the natural growth of a Fibonacci spiral – in the same pattern, the foliage of a shrub grows around a stem to receive optimum sunlight to illuminate the spirit of the clients and customers.

A lotus organisation might need to be on constant alert that it does not mutate into the lotus-eaters' *Nymphaea stellata* and become self-indulgent, laid-back, languid and disinclined to move ahead. This lotus structure is ideal for a building project's professional team's multidisciplined organisation. The client, architect and all the senior specialist team members would be located in the central command flower. The project manager, construction manager and the on-site specialist's staff are located in the surrounding leaf pods with direct access to the central control and everyone is readily aware of the goal and intended outcome.

When an architect is appointed to design a project for a client's organisation, the architect needs to know and understand the culture and ethos of the organisation. When taking a brief, to get an in-depth insight into the client's needs, the art of listening is to hear what the client is not saying.

Works cited

R. Fagles trans. *Homer: The Odyssey*, Penguin Classic, London, 1997.

Peter Drucker. *The Practice of Management*, Routledge, London, 2007.

CHAPTER 21

ETHICS

The teaching and practice of architecture raise questions about our modern standards of ethics and morals in all our dealings, including business and politics. Whether the organisation is a national government, a local authority, a corporate entity, a small business enterprise or the way we run and manage our own lives, these positive and negative archetypes symbolise the fundamental characteristics and principles present in all good and bad forms of governance and our own personal boundaries.

Teaching ethics, business management, leadership, business administration, corporate organisation, marketing, and so on, is a vast global business. William F. Buckley Jr, prominent conservative journalist and founder of the *National Review*, said, 'I am obliged to confess I should sooner live in a society governed by the first two thousand names in the Boston telephone directory than in a society governed by the two thousand faculty members of Harvard University.'

Several millennia before the fourth century BC's Golden Age of Greek philosophy, the divine unity of the universe and the keys to understanding life and the psycho/spiritual make-up of human nature were taught orally. Greek ethics, as a guiding philosophy or moral principle, are usually high on the curriculum in universities and schools of business and political science. Our leaders learn that Plato's and Aristotle's ethics were concepts of personal happiness and well-being (*eudaimonia*) and leading the good life based on the highest good and the principles of the cardinal virtues (*arête* or excellence) – prudence, wisdom, courage, fortitude, temperance and justice.

At one end of the spectrum is the philosophy of Socrates, and his ethical virtues, expressed as a spiritually flourishing life of self-responsibility, self-control, courage, justice and wisdom: *public good rests on private virtue*. It was not the pursuit of wealth, reputation or success.

On the other hand, according to Democritus, *ethics* is the concern of one's personal happiness and leading a hedonistic, good life – provided of course that you were neither a slave nor a low-caste Athenian. Whereas *morals* were an entirely separate and public issue. In other words, one's ethical, personal responsibilities, way of private life and sense of wisdom and spirituality had no bearing on the way you conducted your affairs of business, politics and the governance of the state. (Nothing new there then.)

These extremes of black or white, left wing or right wing, remain embedded in today's culture. We are wrongly taught that the antithesis of virtue is vice; and bravery is the antithesis of cowardliness. A. C. Grayling, in his recent book on philosophy, points out that virtue lies between the two vices of miserliness and extravagance; and Jeremy Naydler adds that bravery (or courage) lies between cowardliness and fearlessness. The highlighting of these language misnomers may signal embryonic changes in the air that could set a course towards the Dalai Lama's philosophy in his book *The Middle Way*.

About 400 years after the Golden Age of the Greeks, a man known as Thiruvalluvar was born in 31 BC at Tamil Nadu. He wrote *Tamil Marai* in verses of 1,330 couplets and, except for the Bible and the Quran, it is the world's most translated work. This great work sees ethics, morals and human nature as fundamental to the everyday life of the individual, the family, community, society and the state – the fundamental ethos of architecture. The book is a treatise on our basic needs – food, protection, sleep and sex – and our innate quest to become a fully realised human being. It emphasises that the personal standards of ethics, morals and spirituality in our lives are our sole responsibilities and the very foundation in all that we do day-by-day in our personal and business lives. It is the essence of humanism and the sanctity of life.

Thiruvalluvar is still held in high esteem and revered in Tamil Nadu, one of the most developed and cultured states in India. On 1 January 2000, a statue of him was unveiled off the coast of his birthplace, Kanyakumari. It is built on a rock, 133 feet high, as a symbolic reference to the 1,330 verses. The *Kural*, as this great work is known, is rarely taught in schools of business and political science.

Carl J. Schramm, who has been called the 'Evangelist of Entrepreneurship' by *The Economist*, believes that business plans should be burned because the management theories, techniques and strategies taught by academics and theorists only serve to retard entrepreneurship and enterprise. Of course, the study of ethics, business systems, technical tools and aids are useful but even the Bank of England acknowledged that its management should rely less on spreadsheets and the London economists (academics) and more on the views of the folk wisdom of so-called ordinary people.

Works cited

A. C. Grayling. *The History of Philosophy*, Penguin Viking, 2019.

Jeremy Naydler. *In the Shadow of the Machine*, Temple Lodge, 2018.

The Dalai Lama. *The Middle Way: Faith Grounded in Reason*, Wisdom Publications, Boston, 2014.

Thiruvalluvar, trans. Richa Prakashan. *Thirukkural*, Richa Prakashan, 2005

Carl J. Schramm. *Burn the Business Plan: What Great Entrepreneurs Really Do*, John Murray Learning London, 2018.

PART IV

THOUGHTS ON MYTHS AND MANAGEMENT

CHAPTER 22
MYTHS, FOLK WISDOM AND ARCHETYPES

'Myth is always the unconscious representation of such crucial life situations, and one of the reasons why myths are so significant for us is that we can read the true experiences of mankind in these confessions unobscured by consciousness.' So said psychologist Erich Neumann in *Amor and Psyche*, speaking of 'the marriage situation as an archetype and central figure of feminine psychic reality'. When we open our eyes for the first time, we are in a state of bliss and at one with the world. All too soon, we have to come to terms with survival, disease and crime, poverty and riches, personal relationships, business and politics, life and death. How these concepts and conditions control our attitudes to personal responsibilities and other people, to society in general, the planet Earth, and the invisible universe, depends on how we relate to ourselves. These are the ethical and moral challenges that balance our natural instincts for survival and the desire for gratification with the need to have a deeper understanding of the world about us.

You are the hero of your own life's story
'Choose a job you love, and you will never have to work a day

in your life,' said Confucius. All love affairs need reciprocal relationships that nurture aspirations and encourage growth to develop and continue to enhance love and respect. Your relationship with the people you work with and for, as well as the workplace environment and culture, will be a determining effect on how your love affair will flourish and inspire your life.

Whatever the chosen job, training and qualification, your love affair will be engaged in some form of organisation. When you walk into the workplace – an office, shop, studio, factory or building site – your psyche will subconsciously register what goes on, how the organisation works, who reports to whom and who does what. Whether the organisation is large, small or a one-person enterprise, it will be led, managed and staffed. Who are these people, what do they do, what are their characteristics and what makes them tick? It is easier to answer these questions when we let go of our rational mind's mode of thinking based on reductionism, literalism and scientism and, instead, depend on our intuitive mind to see, hear, feel and understand what is innately sensed and perceived.

Folk wisdom stories

Cultures throughout history have created mythological stories that explore the unknown to guide and explain how we can come to terms with the chaos and uncertainty of life and living. Said Albert Einstein, 'If you want your children to be intelligent, read them fairy tales. If you want your children to be more intelligent, read them more fairy tales.' Before modern psychology, perennial folk wisdom stories were at the heart of esoteric teachings expressing universal truths that belong to no one race, creed or culture. These stories and their archetypal characters are the symbolic, mystical expressions of the primal nature of human beings. Fundamentally, they follow the same underlying themes and principles of the unseen forces of light and dark within us that can transform our life and relationships. It is through these sacred tales that we learn about natural phenomena, human nature and cultural or social truths that can influence our own heroic journey in life. The mythological gods and goddesses, kings, queens, warriors, magicians, witches and warlocks, giants and dragons in classic fairy tales represent universal patterns of human behaviour. These archetypal characters express eternal ideas, instantly recognised and intuitively understood by the psyche. They also depict some of the sub-personalities hidden in the shadows of our mind. They are aspects of the same characters and situations we experience every day in TV dramas, films, plays, video games, chess and games of snakes and ladders.

Another profound philosophy, again based on the ancient perennial wisdom of esoteric teachings on ethics, morals and human nature, first appeared in medieval Europe in the form of a forgotten language as a picture 'book' of cards known as the *Ancien Tarot de Marseille*. (Bear in mind that throughout most periods in history, the vast majority of the population could neither read nor write.) The pictographs of the arcane images of archetypal principles and insights are an ethical guide to self-understanding and awareness. Unlike many hundreds of other Tarot packs, this unique, authentic deck was not devised for fortune telling but was an arcane book of esoteric knowledge of our life's journey from naivety to wisdom. These universal images are the same characters depicted in traditional fairy tales, the allegorical frescoes of Siena, the virtues and vices of Greek philosophy and in the mythical pantheon of Mount Olympus.

The Authentic Tarot: Discovering Your Inner Self by Thomas Saunders decodes the arcane symbolism of the *Ancien Tarot de Marseille* and an extraordinary world of mystical revelation and the rites of initiation from naivety to wisdom. Its profound symbolism reveals our personal path to self-awareness. When, metaphorically, we venture into the *dark, foreboding woods* or a *deep cave*, it is the first step in our quest for self-discovery.

Works cited

Erich Neumann. *Amor and Psyche: the Psychic Development of the Feminine*, Routledge, London, 1956.

Thomas Saunders. *The Authentic Tarot: Discovering Your Inner Self*, Watkins Publishing, 2007.

CHAPTER 23
THE ALLEGORICAL FRESCOES

University and business school academics who teach political sciences and MBA (Master of Business Administration) courses, all their current students, graduates and everyone, including architects, project managers and everyone running an organisation, should go to Siena, Italy for an extensive, detailed, in-depth field study of the business and political ethics in the profound symbolism of the Allegorical Frescoes of Good and Bad Government by Ambrogio Lorenzetti. (Academics should get out more in any case.) There, in the Council Chamber of the Palazzo Pubblico, they will clearly see the stark realities of good and bad leadership, management and governance, and witness the positive outcome in contrast to the disastrous consequences of an autocratic, despotic regime. (Despotism is only a goosestep away from tyranny).

In the ninth century, six hundred years after the collapse of the Roman Empire, the Italian peninsular was under the control of its major cities. Within five hundred years, Venice, Florence, Milan and Siena had developed into powerful, wealthy, independent Republican city states and cultural centres. Their rivalry and competitiveness occasionally spilled over into armed conflict.

During the thirteenth and fourteenth centuries, Siena established the first bank – Banca Monte dei Paschi de Siena (which still exists today) – and its citizens continued to reap the benefits of a secure, well-run government. In Florence, Lorenzo de' Medici created the world's first Academy of Art in his Orsini Palace, where Michelangelo and other great artists were students. At the same time, in medieval England, despite the Magna Carta of 1215, feudalism was still prevalent and the landed barons carried on fighting the divine right of the king to redress the injustices in land ownership. But nothing changed for the general citizens; serfdom continued and the laws of legacy excluded Jews and widows. A few years later, the political unrest led to the Peasants' Revolt.

Siena's Gothic-style Palazzo Pubblico (the Town Hall, and now a museum) was built at the southeastern end of the Piazza del Campo in 1297 and completed in 1308. Twenty years later, the Campanile was added to rival the one in Florence. (Same syndrome today – my tower is bigger than yours). The Palazzo housed the extensive council meeting rooms and offices. Tucked away on the first floor is the modest 10m x 16m council chamber called Sala della Pace – the Hall of Peace. It was also called the Sala dei Nove – the Council of Nine – which became the longest form of government to rule Siena during the period of its greatest development.

The frescoes

Allegory a story, poem or picture that can be interpreted to reveal a hidden meaning, typically a moral, political or religious idea.

In 1337, Siena's enlightened councillors – nobles, traders and ordinary folk – commissioned Ambrogio Lorenzetti to paint non-religious allegories in the Sala dei Nove to express their political philosophy and ideals. The frescoes graphically illustrate the outcome of good and bad government. They highlight the axiom that a picture is worth a thousand words; they are indeed worth millions of words, oral teachings and written instructions.

The frescoes' characters speak to us in the covert symbolic language of the archetypes found in myths and fairy tales that are embedded in our DNA and intuitively recognised and understood by the psyche. According to Carl Jung, who coined the term 'collective unconscious':

> Symbolism of the enigmatic characters and numbers represent something else by association or convention that expresses an inner dimension that has layers of meaning understood more by the unconscious rather than the conscious mind. Archetypes are a collectively inherited unconscious idea, pattern of thought, image etc. universally present in individual psyches.

When you enter the council chamber, look up at the frieze and you will be confronted by the domain of Bad Government commanded by a satanic *Tyrant*. The scales of *Justice* are broken; *Peace* lies dead at his feet; the menacing *Avarice*, *Betrayal*, and the *Vices* complete the scenes of chaos, fear and destruction. The deserted buildings in the city are dilapidated and open to crime; the countryside is uncultivated and armies are lined up for battle. There is an air of violence and the citizens are ignored and unprotected.

Opposite the single window, look to the right and the fresco depicts the noble king-like figure of *Securitas* (Security) representing the Council of Nine Magistrates. Above his crown are the guiding qualities of *Faith*, *Hope* and *Charity*; alongside him are the Virtues – on his left are *Temperance* and *Magnanimity* with a crowned *Justice* holding her upright sword. On his left, *Peace, Fortitude* and *Prudence* stand over the guards and soldiers protecting the citizens.

On the left of the frieze, and transcending all, is the angel of *Divine Wisdom* over the main figure of *Justice* with the scales of punishment on her right and *Concord* on her left. A symbolic thread connects the seated figure of the *Common Good* and the procession of the twenty-four elected councillors.

The frieze above the entrance door and facing the Tyrant are the frescoes of Good Government. The city walls are in good order; the streets are alive with dancers and a wedding procession; the traders are thriving and builders are working on the houses. In the countryside, the farms are well tended, irrigated and planted; people and animals are freely roaming the fields.

The RIBA's motto – *Service for the citizens and the glory of the city* – expresses the ideals and aspirations of Siena's Council of Nine.

Works cited

C. G. Jung. *The Archetypes and the Collective Unconscious.* Routledge London, 1991

CHAPTER 24
MEET THE ARCHETYPES

The word *arche* is the first principle. It is eternal, ageless and the elemental genesis of all reality and appearances. Archetypal images of the feminine and masculine principles are present in varying degrees in both women's and men's psyches. We all have a variety of archetypal characters embedded in our psyche that serve as members of a board of directors: their instinctive trends or underlying characteristics can dominate, interchange and emerge at different periods in our life. They are not rigid stereotypes for labelling other people.

Archetypes   A collectively inherited unconscious idea, pattern of thought, image…universally present in individual psyches. (C. G. Jung)

The female archetypes
Jennifer Barker Woolger and Roger Woolger's book *The Goddess Within* explores aspects of the female psyche in the six goddesses in the pantheon of Greek mythology – Hera, Persephone, Athena, Artemis, Demeter, Aphrodite. Their counterparts in brackets are characters found in the *Ancien Tarot de Marseille*.

The Goddess Hera (Tarot's the Empress)

Hera, the Empress of Olympus, represents the collective consciousness of the tangible world. As the traditional wife, upholding marriage, morality and relationships, she will always accept the infidelities of her husband, the Emperor Zeus, provided she continues to retain a share of his power and political control. (Think Hillary Clinton.) In her negative mode she can be the wicked witch and terrible, devouring mother (Cinderella's stepmother). When her overbearing, strident love of power turns obsessive, she can indulge in political intrigue and misuse her authority.

The Goddess Persephone (Tarot's Force)

Persephone lives in the underworld (Hades) during the winter and re-emerges in the springtime. She is the psychic guide to healing, the occult, visions and transformations, and holds the power of unconscious forces and sacred magic. (Think Dr Candace Pert 1946–2013, author of *Molecules of Emotion*.) Persephone's psychic instincts can turn to black magic and mischief.

The Goddess Athena (Tarot's Justice)

Athena represents clarity of mind, intellectual independence, civil liberties and civilisation. Her qualities of leadership, sense of responsibility and duty demands order and respect. She can create harmony and fairness. Her innate wisdom ranges from culture and education to rebellion and waging war. (Think Baroness Margaret Thatcher, 1925–2013, prime minister and barrister). In her negative mode, she has powers of logic and reason that can manipulate situations to satisfy her own ends, resulting in chaos, untruths and dishonour.

The Goddess Artemis (Tarot's the Star)

Artemis' epithets are the hunting bull goddess, queen of the beasts, and the Moon goddess. She is the guardian of the flora and fauna of the forest and fiercely protects and defends nature with her bow and arrows. Artemis is the independent adventurer and hunter who is at home in the wilderness. Her form of independence can develop a distrust of men and her own body wisdom. You will find her campaigning for climate change and the World Wildlife Fund or fighting ivory poachers, running a sheep farm, a stray dogs' home or working on TV's *Country File.* (Think political activist Emmeline Pankhurst, 1858–1928, or primatologist and conservationist Dian Fossey, 1932–1985, of *Gorillas in the Mist* fame.)

The Goddess Demeter (Tarot's Temperance)

Demeter is Mother Earth, the goddess of agriculture, harvests, fertility, sustenance and the natural cycles of life and death. She also represents the life force, compassion, childbirth and the nurturing of young ones to grow and mature. (Think Queen Victoria surrounded by her nine children.) Demeter is the protector of the family and keeps the home fires burning. In her negative mode she can be the overpowering, overprotective mother who prevents children from growing up and leaving home.

The Goddess Aphrodite (Tarot's the World)

Aphrodite personifies feminine intuition, love, sexuality, passion and the outer world of sensuality. She is a lover of the arts, architecture, fashion and creativity. She can transform the house into an elegant, beautifully decorated home. It is Aphrodite who has a vase of flowers on her desk and dresses up, well perfumed, to go out dancing. She takes care of the pleasures of life and the qualities of the environment. In her negative mode, she can become the seductress, indulging in starry-eyed intrigue and narcissism. Her jealousies can create chaos. (Think Lucrezia Borgia 1480–1519.)

Erich Neumann was a student of Carl Jung. In his influential book *Amor and Psyche: The Psychic Development of the Feminine* he explores the relationship and conflict between Aphrodite, her son Amor (Eros) and the mortal Psyche. It is a commentary on the story of Cupid and Psyche in Apuleius' Roman classic *The Golden Ass*, which expresses invaluable insights into a woman's intuition and creativity. We discover Aphrodite's negative modes and the eventual release of her spoilt son to allow him to grow up. It also tells us more about Hera, Demeter and Persephone.

The male archetypes

Joseph Campbell's book *The Hero with a Thousand Faces* interprets the many guises of the archetypal folklore of the Hero. In their book *King, Warrior, Magician, Lover,* Robert Moore and Douglas Gillette explore the masculine psyche. These same symbolic characters and characteristics can be seen in the *Ancien Tarot de Marseille* deck, which is discussed in *The Authentic Tarot*.

The Hero King (Tarot's the Emperor)

The King – the wise old man – represents the masculine principles of rationality, an earthy nature, stability and material attainment. He is the leader and the titular head who has authority and power, and commands law and order. He will inspire, encourage and bless his subjects, mete out fair justice and, together with the Empress, protect boundaries and provide security to the realm. (Think Alfred the Great, King of Wessex 871–886 and the Siena fresco *Securitas*.) The King's leadership is also a marriage between intuitive, instinctive thoughts and intellectual thinking. He performs his duty to serve, not to exercise power over others. He fears nothing from man, beast or the gods, and his realm lives in peace, harmony and collaboration in life. In his dysfunctional mode he can become the all-powerful, evil Tyrant with overburdening egotistical pride and hubris. He will tend to blame and condemn others. (Think the Siena fresco Tyrant.)

The Hero/Heroine Warrior (Tarot's Charioteer)

The Warrior personifies the courageous Hero/Heroine/ Knight in shining armour. Warriors are the astronauts and armed forces; the competitive sportsmen and women; farmers; traders; and the architects and engineers who build things. When Warriors leave the protection of Mother and Father to face the exposure and responsibilities of adulthood (transition) they allow intuition and instinct to guide them to act with magnanimity, sensitivity, integrity and faithfulness. Courage is needed to release the reins, commit to the quest and venture into unknown, uncharted territory. They are out on their own and need to be prepared to deal with unpleasant surprises, accepting conflict as essential for growth. (Think Isambard Brunel, Lord Nelson, Boudicca, Florence Nightingale, Hugues de Payens, founder of the Knights Templar and Jeanne d'Arc.) Without balance and purpose they will aimlessly charge or wander about and become the cruel sadist, masochist, bully and conceited coward.

The Hero Magician (Tarot's the Magician)

The Magician represents the clever, resourceful innovator and imaginative visionary and planner with infinite potential. Architects, engineers, mathematicians, scientists, researchers, the code breakers of Bletchley Park, the inventor Q in the James Bond films, the shaman, the witch doctor and healers – they are all Magicians. (Think Alan Turing, 1912–1954, code breaker at Bletchley Park and inventor of the computer.) Magicians in their negative mode can become dark-web computer hackers, confidence tricksters, the cheating manipulators who misuse power and indulge in black magic and charlatanism. They will always profess innocence.

The Hero Lover (Tarot's the Lover and the Hermit)

The Hero Lover is the poet, painter and champion of the environment, ecology and nature. (Think Sir David Attenborough.) The Lover has an appetite for life and the sensuous pleasures of the mind and body in relationships. Often, he is likely to find himself at the crossroads having to choose which path to follow to connect his spiritual life with his emotional life to reach harmony to become whole and complete. If his early childhood and youth has been dominated by powerful males and females, he may become super-sensitive and resent any demands to conform or exercise disciplined thoughts and actions. This will develop the negative mode of Puer Aeternus – Peter Pan, the eternal child – and retract into a naïve, unrealistic dreamer and impotent weakling: the Don Juan and drug addict.

According to Robert Bly, leader of the mythopoetic men's movement, the naive weaklings:

- Will lose what is most precious because they know no boundaries
- Have special relationships but never question or recognise their own *shadow*
- Will pick up the pain of others
- Will not follow instructions
- Find their timing is always off
- Believe everyone is honest, sincere and speaks from the heart

Negative Lovers are those who never make mistakes and take orders from those who do.

Meet the players

The leaders and managers
Archetypal images: *Hera, the Empress, Athena, the Emperor, the Magician.*

Their tasks are to deal with the organisation's strategy and tactics, protect the culture, ethics, and style of the business, and to be of service to the client. They are not there to instruct but to guide and encourage the talents and abilities of others.

The front-line staff
Archetypal images: *Athena, Artemis, Warrior, Charioteer.*

These are the meeters and greeters and joiners – the people in sales, marketing and the on-site team, ever-ready to pack a bag and travel to make things happen and get things done.

The backroom staff
Archetypal images: *Persephone, Magician.*

These are the creative wizards who produce the inventive magic for the front-line staff to sell, market and build.

The welfare staff

Archetypal images: *Demeter, Aphrodite, Justice, Temperance, the Star, the Lover, the Hermit.*

These are the environmentalists, ecologists and protectors of the likely adverse impacts of what the others are planning to do.

Promotion

In our employment culture, usually the only way a good, talented schoolteacher can improve his or her income and status is to stop teaching and become an administrator as the head of the school. When a Magician is promoted to the role of a Warrior or vice versa, depending on the individual, it can be stressful and a waste of innate teaching abilities. On the other hand, the challenge could be an exhilarating and life-enhancing experience. The ideal job is one that is valuable to oneself and society as well as being a pleasurable and sustainable activity that matches one's unexplored talents and abilities.

Postscript

With apologies to Jacques' speech in Shakespeare's *As You Like It* (Act II Scene VII):

> All the world's a revolving business stage,
> And all the women and men merely players;
> Acting out the archetypes' many parts.
> At first Hera the Empress and King the

Emperor enter the stage,
Dressed as the Chief Executives in their high
heels and polished lace-up shoes.
They speak with their Managers about
strategy and tactics, culture and ethics
And being of service to their staff, clients and
customers.
Then the scene changes and Athena, Artemis
and the Warrior appear,
Armed for travel, with pull-on luggage, train
and plane tickets, hard hats and boots,
Carrying plans, sales and marketing
brochures, ready to meet and greet their
clients.
And next, Persephone and the Magician
enter stage left.
The studio, workshop, and office is quietly
busy with designers, inventors,
accountants and lawyers.
The stage turns again. Demeter, Aphrodite
and the Lover, all casually dressed,
Staring at the staff welfare wall charts,
scrutinising the environmental impacts
On the organisation's plans.
And so, they have all played their parts, ready
to act again
In this strange, eventful comedy that keeps
turning: Sans time.

Works cited

C. G. Jung. *The Archetypes and the Collective Unconscious*, Routledge, London, 1991.

Jennifer Barker Woolger, Roger J. Woolger. *The Goddess Within*, Rider, London, 1990.

Erich Neumann. *Amor and Psyche: The Psychic Development of the Feminine*, Princeton University Press, 1971.

Lucius Apuleius, trans. Robert Graves. *The Golden Ass*, Penguin Classics, London.

Robert Moore, Douglas Gillette. *King, Warrior, Magician, Lover*, HarperCollins Publishers, 1991.

Suggested further reading

Sallie Nichols. *Jung and the Tarot: An Archetypal Journey*, Samuel Weiser, 1984.

Robert Bly. *Iron John: A Book about Men*, Addison-Wesley Publishing, 1990.

Joseph Campbell. *The Hero With a Thousand Faces*, Paladin Grafton Books, 1988.

Thomas Saunders. *The Authentic Tarot: Discovering Your Inner Self*, Watkins Publishing, 2017.

PART V

AFTERTHOUGHTS

CHAPTER 25
TODAY'S CHALLENGES

It could be said that today's nadir of the profession's status began with the early nineteenth century's culture of materialism. A belief that materialism and the physical body are the only realities fosters the expectation that anything and everything – disease, natural calamities, food production, global warming and environmental disasters – can be overcome and cured by advanced technology. But since the West abandoned the soul and dismissed the sacred in favour of the profane, and globalisation, it has inevitably led to being at war with nature and its deconstruction. As Goethe said, 'Ignorant men raise questions that wise men answered a thousand years ago.'

The Campaign to Protect Rural England has reported that more than half the population of England struggle to see stars in the sky due to light pollution. This loss of connection with the natural world cannot be experienced through virtual reality by looking at a TV screen, laptop or mobile phone. It is also detrimental to our health. Despite its many benefits, technical progress has created environmental conditions that are potentially detrimental to our well-being. Maybe we have already passed the point where our ingenuity can 'fix it' by inventing even more technology to counter the previous technological problems, because technology tends to exacerbate rather than resolve difficulties. Our faith in materialism, technology, consumerism and market forces has not brought us any nearer to our goal of health, happiness and prosperity.

Author Beredene Jocelyn was an exponent of Rudolf Steiner's anthroposophic philosophy. In her book, *Citizens of the Cosmos*, she writes:

> The time has come to think not only in terms of natural laws, but also in accordance with planetary laws that affect us as threefold beings of body, soul and spirit. By doing so, we attune ourselves consciously to cosmic rhythms and feel related to the cosmos as well as to our earthly environment. When we see the disorder Man is creating, it is encouraging to know that order does exist in the cosmos. We can be sure that the sun will not rise a minute or even seconds late. In proportion to our recognition and application of cosmic laws, order will be restored in individual lives and in earthly affairs.

The profession of architecture is not short of the material and the teachers to counter the one-sided mechanistic functionalism and 'soullessness' that is often expressed in the modern built environment. All that is needed is the necessary will and understanding to change. The teaching and practice of architecture reflects the aspects of a secular culture that is compartmentalised, fragmented and separated from our relationship with the Earth and the universal laws of nature.

Mainstream traditions of the North European Megalithic and Asian Bronze and Iron Age architects were passed on to the esoteric schools that continued through the Celtic tradition to the present day. Mystery school teachings were the basis of the fundamental principles of the location, design and construction of the magnificent architecture of the Egyptian, Greek, Roman, Gothic and Renaissance periods, including the great buildings of Islam in the Middle East and India. Whatever the style, period or function, these ancient principles integrating and cooperating with natural energies and cosmic order are still more or less covertly practised in many parts of the world.

The universal source of philosophy, metaphysics, art and science (including 'doing the drawings') attributed to the practices of the bygone master architects, appear to have been drawn from the ancient mystery school teachings that have always been available, albeit covertly. These fundamental teachings and practice are the essence and values of architecture *with* architects. The master architects were leaders and innovators who dedicated their life and work to designing buildings and the built environment according to the fundamental principles of the sacred arts and sciences to create architecture to symbolise a spiritual, mystical concept expressing people's relationship with the underlying laws or canon of nature and the cosmos. Their *knowledge* and *understanding* was the built environment's impact on the citizen's health, well-being and spiritual life.

It appears that throughout history, from the architects of the pyramids of Giza and the Mayan temples, to the master builders of Chartres cathedral, to Palladio and other great masters of the Renaissance, and twentieth- and twenty-first century architects, human beings have endeavoured to make this connection. Why now, do we tend to disregard perennial wisdom and devalue thousands of years of human knowledge?

According to the director emeritus of the Institute of Traditional Studies, Robert C. Meurant:

> [Architecture] in our modern secular Western culture suffers from the absence of a suitable Metaphysic [...] Different aspects of being are regarded as being detached from one another – a situation of virtual dimensional degradation. Thus the metaphysical aspect of architecture is often seen as being irrelevant to the theory and practice of architecture; and therefore [is] seen in isolation and not naturally situated within a metaphysical context. Relevance and meaning are made subordinate to political influence and expediency at the expense of Truth...and we are neglecting it through ignorance of our true nature – it is inevitable that our architecture should become [...] impoverished. [It] needs to be derived from transcendental principles.

Has metaphysics any relevance to the Western civilisation of the twenty-first century, and if so, are we interested? The world has never been short of wise sages and fundamental spiritual teachings, but we have been too caught up in materialism to want to listen. Today, as ever, there are masters who have the knowledge, vision and passion to manifest an architecture that expresses the perennial principles of harmony, beauty and truth. They are still with us.

There have always been periods in history when human beings have struggled to come to terms with the conflict between reason and inner knowingness; between intuition and logic; between religion, spirituality and science; between the sacred and the profane; and our relationship and interconnectedness with nature and the cosmos. It is acutely so now. Instead of searching for meaning and understanding the purpose of life, our destiny and the mysteries of death, we expend our preciously short time and energy on trying to discover new transient things to distract our thoughts away from the transcendental. It is we, the society of 'ordinary citizens', who must look beyond the mundane – the profane – and place materialism and actuality in their proper context in terms of holism. Why does our current mind-set recognise only a material world of the senses? And yet, we know instinctively and intuitively there is more to life than simply earning a living, keeping ourselves and our family physically sustained, and continually striving to satisfy the senses.

Mathematician and philosopher Alfred North Whitehead said that science was blind because it dealt with only part of the evidence of human experience and there was much more to the world of atomic matter. Physicist Max Planck concluded that beyond the subatomic realm yet another world of reality existed beyond our present world of sense, and according to physicist Werner Heisenberg, in the atomic (material) realm, atoms are more than 'things'. In other words there is something else because there is no distinction between matter and energy. Theoretical physicists have a profound sense of mysticism where 'reality' is transcendent and impermanent, but entirely interrelated with a whole spectrum of realities from the gross physical world to the subtle metaphysical realms. When they attempt to describe the realities from the infinitesimally small world of subatomic particles to the infinitely vast realms of astrophysics, the words are far more familiar to the language of metaphysical poets, transcendental philosophers and the esoteric teachings of perennial wisdom.

Subatomic physics has opened the window on to a phenomenal, almost incredible universe and many areas of modern science repeatedly confirm the view held by the ancient seers of 'as above, so below'. Further 'evidence' of a spiritual dimension has come from a most unexpected quarter – the scientific community itself that for so long has focused exclusively on the physical and discounted the metaphysical concepts of nature and reality. Perhaps inadvertently, the trend was reversed in the latter half of the twentieth century by those physicists who have searched for fundamental particles and the elusive Theory of Everything.

The discovery of anti-protons in 1955 by Professor Emilio Segrè and Dr Owen Chamberlain revealed that the universe consists of normal atomic matter, but within the atom there exist subatomic particles comprising protons, which have mass – touchable matter – and anti-protons, which have no mass. The non-mass world of light and colour interpenetrates the world of matter. Einstein proved that although protons exist they do not exist in time but have an infinite life.

In *The Elegant Universe,* Professor Brian Greene set out his string (superstring) theory to unify the existence and behaviour of everything from the smallest particles to galaxies. Inside quarks, gluons, photons and neutrinos are tiny 'strings' that vibrate in patterns as if, according to Greene, the cosmos were a 'shimmering Aeolian harp' where each electron plays one note and the quark plays another. Are these notes a continuum of Pythagoras' music of the spheres?

In Western society a way of life is emerging that is reacting to pure materialism. Presently in the West we are re-examining all spheres of existence – from both human and spiritual standpoints – in a totally unprecedented way. This re-examination is a desire (both conscious and unconscious) to reconnect with the spiritual dimension of our being, and presents the wider public and ourselves with an opportunity to become 'informed clients'. The majority of so-called ordinary people are highly receptive to innovative, avant-garde modern architecture. When we enter a building or arrive at a particular location, we commonly experience intuitive insights that may be either enjoyable or uncomfortable sensations. Architects and all their fellow professionals are encouraged to be original and inventive and, at the same time, to ensure that modern technology and its short-term improvements do not have a negative impact on our long-term health and quality of life. Certainly, we do not want buildings and our cities to be soulless and barren.

Can our perception of the universe and our relationship to it be expressed in our modern society and the built environment? Written thousands of years ago, the basic tenet of the ancient Hindu scriptures known as the Vedas (a Sanskrit word meaning 'divine knowledge') is that everything in the universe – the galaxies, stars, planets and all living organisms – has a life force, a consciousness, and that everything interacts with everything else. The ancients respected the Earth as an intelligent, living entity as much alive as every cell in our body.

The web of vibration and how we interact with the Earth energy fields, cosmic forces, electromagnetic fields, light, colour, sound, and the philosophy, physics and metaphysics of life, are neither taught in the schools of architecture nor understood by the majority of practising architects. This leaves to chance whether a building and the built environment will be disturbing, inherently sick, and detrimental to all those in occupation, or whether it will be spiritually uplifting and conducive to health and well-being.

If we are to get the architecture we need and want, then the twenty-first century's architects need to have the skills, knowledge and understanding of nature and the natural world, the human psyche, biology and the endocrine glands, the planetary influences on Earth energy and electromagnetic fields, colour vibrations, sound, light pollution, and people's love of place and abode.

The legacy of perennial wisdom and our innate intuition sets out to heighten our awareness and offer guidance on practical solutions to all those engaged in the built environment in order to challenge a one-dimensional, materialistic and compartmentalised view of humanity and nature. Whether we are students, teachers, practising professional architects, or from any other walk of life, we need an understanding of the fundamental realities of the universe and how we relate to it to create healthy, soul-enriching environments that are fit for human habitation. The ethos of the ancient architects was to be of *service for the citizens and the glory of the city.*

Works cited

Robert C. Meurant. *The Aesthetics of the Sacred*, Opoutere Press, Auckland, 1985.

Beredene Jocelyn. *Citizens of the Cosmos*, Continuum, New York, 1981.

Brian Greene. *The Elegant Universe*, W.W. Norton, 1999.

CHAPTER 26

INTUITION AND THE ART OF KNOWING

'The intuitive mind is a sacred gift. The rational mind is a reliable servant. We have created a society that welcomes the servant and has forgotten the gift.'

Albert Einstein

A TV wildlife documentary tracked a herd of elephants for miles as they searched for water in dried up scrubland. After several days in the arid terrain, they came to a dusty patch of land, skirted around the area, prodding the dirt with their trunks, and then began to pound the earth. They dug to a depth of about two metres and suddenly water seeped into the hole. Soon, the elephants and other animals were drinking and bathing in a deep pool somewhere in the vast, parched Serengeti plain. In *Beyond Supernature*, marine biologist and zoologist Dr Lyall Watson provides a biophysical explanation for the many examples of animals having extraordinary sensitivity to water and their ability to find underground sources at times of drought.

Schools of whales, shoals of salmon, flights of migrating birds and other creatures, including insects, use their equivalent of the pineal gland to navigate the Earth's magnetic radiation to return to their nests and breeding grounds. Eels are spawned in the North Atlantic's Sargasso Sea, then swarm to live in fresh inland waters before returning to the ocean to spawn and die.

Deer, mice and pheasants, among other creatures, habitually move along certain tracks and pathways. In his book *The Pattern of the Past*, Guy Underwood suggests that so-called ley lines are a concentration of subtle Earth currents of electromagnetic or electrostatic fields. Why do some locations, such as the Rollright Stones in Oxfordshire, and certain buildings of whatever age, whether religious or secular, induce psychic experiences or a sense of well-being and feelings of being in touch with the spirit of the natural world? Infrared thermometers can detect and measure the changing spectrum of a location's energy field and where geological fault lines occur; a clockwise spin will have a positive resonance with the human body and the release of certain endocrine gland secretions. Ancient sites and medieval cathedrals were built precisely over a well or crossing underground streams. On the other hand, at a location where there is an anti-clockwise or negative spin, the interference pattern of the energy field will create an opposite and harmful effect. Infrared aerial photography carried out over the medieval town of Regensburg in Sweden in 1981 showed that the ancient meandering streets follow precisely the lines of subterranean water courses. Was it coincidental or by accident that all the buildings were located away from the potentially harmful stress rays created by the underground streams?

Before modern science developed an array of specialised techniques such as infrared photography, terrestrial radar, geomagnetometers, Geiger counters, seismic meters, ultrasonic and microwave detectors, how on Earth – so to speak – did the ancient architects and master geomancers detect positive and harmful energy fields, electromagnetic telluric currents, and subterranean streams and springs? How did the Greeks and Romans locate geological fault lines to install anti-seismic barriers?

The innate ability of human beings to accurately detect and evaluate Earth energies and geophysical properties of the land is the age-old art or science of dowsing – sometimes called *divining*. Dowsers often describe it is as 'the art of knowing'.

Prehistoric cave paintings, ancient Egyptian hieroglyphics and sculptures, biblical writings, medieval woodcuts and other historical documents show dowsing as a usual means for finding sources of water and tracking Earth energy fields. Vitruvius wrote detailed instructions on the various methods he used to find a source of water. However, in the sixteenth century Martin Luther denounced dowsing as the work of the devil, since when the Western world has treated it with caution. (The French translation of 'water spring' is *la source* or *eau de source*: a dowser is known as a *sourcier* or *sorcier*. In English, a *sorcerer* is one who dabbles in black magic.)

The eighteenth-century empress Catherine the Great issued a proclamation that a dowsing rod must be included in the coat of arms of the city of Petrozavodsk. Dowsing, referred to as biolocation, continues to be used extensively in Russia and its Commonwealth of Independent States for finding water and mineral deposits, for archaeology, and for detecting leaks in underground pipework and transcontinental pipelines. During the 1960s the USSR government set up a Ministry of Geology to provide a foundation for the official recognition of dowsing. Research work, practical operations and training programmes continued to highlight the increasing level and widespread dowsing activity being pursued in Russia.

German, French and Austrian medical practitioners use dowsers in their healthcare programmes, and architects and engineers from those countries are trained to locate harmful Earth rays on building sites. Municipal authorities in Poland also have regular training programmes to teach dowsing to student architects and engineers. In rural areas of many parts of the world, it is still commonplace for farmers, builders and architects to use the services of a dowser, or indeed practise dowsing themselves. Many water boards continue to use dowsers. UK and US oil and gas companies also use dowsers to find new drilling locations both on land and at sea, and a few of the major companies are willing to admit that some of the offshore fields have been discovered by dowsers in helicopters or high-flying aircraft.

Dowsers were used in the Vietnam War to find Viet Cong tunnels and hidden arms; dowers were used in the Falklands War to detect 'undetectable' plastic mines; the Ministry of Defence used dowsers to search for anthrax-infected horses during World War 2; the Ministry of Agriculture used dowsers to find swine fever corpses hidden by a farmer; police forces in several countries, including the US and European nations, use dowsers to assist their detective work; and many important archaeological finds have been discovered by dowsing.

Scientists and researchers have put forward several hypotheses to explain how dowsing works. A number of experiments have suggested that the wide spectrum of electric and magnetic fields and electromagnetic radiation can be picked up by the nervous system in the human body. The discovery of tiny magnets inside the human brain indicates that we do indeed have the faculty for navigation by magnetic fields. (The ancient Chinese art and science of acupuncture uses magnets in its healing practices). When dowsing for geological faults, the piezoelectrical discharge caused by the Earth's plates squeezing against each other can also be registered in the brain. Electronic equipment operators are rather more expensive than an expert dowser to detect magnetic Earth energy rays, underground streams or water. Controlled experiments have shown that the experienced dowser can be just as accurate but also carry out the work and produce the results in less time and at a fraction of the cost. It is also cheaper to use a dowser than hire a JCB to find lost pipes.

Where water flows through a pipe or in an underground conduit, minute electrical vibrations are discharged in the range of between 1 and 12Hz. Our brainwaves, operating on a similar frequency, set up a resonance with the flow of water and the experienced dowser has learned to identify particular signals according to a personal set of coding and physical responses. In other words, dowsing is a combination of physical (material) and mental (psychic) responses registered by a natural, neurological reaction in the body. Undoubtedly the brain and all the neurophysiological sensors come into play, particularly the pineal gland as the main receptor.

How dowsing works when searching for archaeological remains and other static inert material such as a buried pipe may be difficult to accept, but everything has a vibrational quality and evidence backed up by personal experience indicates that if we focus our attention, the intuitive mind can achieve the most remarkable insights. In *Dowsing: New Light on an Ancient Art*, Tom Williamson, a geological consultant, wrote about German researchers who suggested that experienced dowsers can detect the low frequency vibrations produced by the geological murmurings of the Earth often found near water-bearing features such as fault lines.

In his book, *The Secret of Life*, the Russian-born French

radio engineer Georges Lakhovsky put forward the view that all living organisms emit and receive radiations and are capable of detecting them. In other words, everyone has the natural ability to dowse. Involuntarily, we constantly receive subtle information from natural phenomena without consciously registering the minute fluctuations in the body that influence our reactions, but the signals are filtered out, otherwise we would be overwhelmed by a constant barrage of information. Even though you may not be conscious of your innate dowsing ability, there are minute reactions in your body when you enter a building or, unknowingly, walk over a subterranean stream.

Dowsing is an acute understanding and response to the faintest signals of natural phenomena. Tools such as bent rods, a pendulum, forked hazel or willow twigs are used to focus our attention and tune into specific details to amplify the signals of whatever we are looking for. The tools can be made of any material because all they do is respond to the minutest movement of the dowser's hand or wrist caused by the nervous system in the arm muscles. Some dowsers experience a gripping sensation in the solar plexus, a twitch in the forearm, or some other indication in the body.

Another method, called map dowsing, otherwise known as remote viewing or knowledge at a distance, seems to defy all logic and reasoning, but there is no doubt that it works with a high degree of accuracy. In *The Electric Shock Book*, astrophysicist Michael Shallis writes:

> Map dowsing is no different from field dowsing. The map is a symbolic representation of the landscape, the landscape is a symbolic representation of a non-material and higher

> reality. The mystery of map dowsing is
> removed once it is recognised that all forms of
> dowsing, including radionics and radiesthesia
> are a means of tapping into the ethereal world,
> which itself is expressed in physical reality and
> then further represented by visual symbols.

Dowsers who have successful track records for locating oil and gas fields at sea or in vast tracts of land, initially tend to use maps to 'traverse' an area before pinpointing the actual drill-rig positions on-site. Sir Geoffroy Tory, a British naval intelligence officer, used remote viewing to locate nuclear submarines. Both the CIA and the KGB trained remote viewers for their Cold War spying exploits, which later proved to have met with considerable success. The respective units were stood down when the Cold War ended. Sadly, due to recent tensions, it is believed that new units have been recruited.

Dowsing is a personal experience of intuition at work. We live in an age when logic and materialistic rationality tend to downgrade, or dismiss outright, the inestimable value of our innate awareness and instincts. Today we refer to 'gut feelings' or something 'not smelling right' rather than our intuitive sense. It needs training and practice as well as a degree of trust in one's own intuitive sense. The more we encourage the development of our intuition (our sixth sense) the more we can begin to listen more carefully to the 'quiet inner voice' and regain our awareness of natural forces. Slight environmental changes in the weather and solar activity can affect the remote-viewer's perceptions.

The essential need to dowse a site for water has largely become obsolete. Since the early twentieth century, the municipal or utility companies have been able to provide reliable records for the location of water mains and other underground utilities. Generally, today's urban architects and engineers rarely concern themselves with the qualities of the Earth's energy fields. Site investigations are mainly limited to investigating soil pollution and the analysis of samples of the subsoil to determine its load-bearing capacity for foundations. The abandonment of dowsing skills has reduced the valuable ability of architects and others engaged in the built environment to discover and take action to neutralise the presence of any harmful energy fields in any new buildings or land for livestock or crops.

Extensive research and certain medical opinions confirm that a connection exists between geobiological Earth radiation and chronic illness. Although certain diseases are not necessarily directly attributable to the location of harmful rays and subterranean water streams, they can trigger the onset of illness by weakening the immune system. Geopathic stress can be described as naturally occurring meandering bands or veins of energy in the form of a faint electrical charge.

Geological fault lines, fissures in the rock formation, mineral seams, and varying strata and subterranean streams flowing in sand or silicone where there will be varying degrees of pressures and geophysical perturbations, can affect the thermic radiation and magnetic field characteristics of a particular place. This unique effect determines whether the 'spin' of a location's energy field is positive or negative and thus creates either benign zones of resonance or malign interference patterns, which impact upon all matter and living organisms. Plants, animals and even minerals react to geopathic stress radiation with increased photon activity. The effect of geopathic radiation on biological organisms became the subject of a Polish state-financed central research programme coordinated by the

Polytechnic in Szczecin (Stettin). The scientific investigation into the harmful effects of subterranean water veins and global grids included various tests to examine the position of the beds of patients who had died of cancer. The results, published in 1989, formed the basis of new guidelines for Polish town planners, architects and construction engineers.

Earlier, in 1961, medical doctor Ernst Hartmann founded the research centre for geobiology (Forschungskreis Für Geobiologie) to study how the human mind, body and soul interacts with the cosmos, the atmosphere, the weather and characteristics of the environment. Hartmann's book *Illness as a Problem of Location* deals with the impact of biophysical forces of the Earth energy fields and artificially generated electromagnetic fields on the body's organs as a source of illnesses and the degeneration or mutation of cells. (Hartmann's work ran parallel to the studies of his associate Herbert L. König, author of *The Invisible Environment*.) Hartmann's work adds to the evidence of Baron Von Pohl's investigative report into the high incidence of cancer in the town of Vilsbiburg in Bavaria where many cancer deaths had been located over strong, geopathic Earth rays. He also discovered that certain animals, plants, insects, parasites, viruses and bacteria are geopathic stress ray seekers.

Dowsing can develop an awareness that can help maintain a healthy, prosperous environment and enhance the ability to detect the subtle Earth energies and forces that can affect our health and sense of well-being. It can heighten our respect for the natural environment. Whether you want to dabble in dowsing as a game of harmless fun or become a professional dowser just to experience the phenomenon of the intuitive mind at work, dowsing increases a conscious awareness of the natural unseen world about us. At the very least, the body becomes sensitive to the Earth's energy fields and the ability to detect and avoid harmful stress lines that may be present in your home or place of work. Experienced dowsers offer a survey service to plot and divert the veins away from the areas where the occupants are most vulnerable.

The legacy of architecture with architects is the intuitive understanding that the Earth is not a lifeless mass of rock and soil and that not anywhere and everywhere is a benign location for buildings, roads and cities. Where tracts of land were unsuitable, dowsers had the knowledge and skills to neutralise the adverse energy fields. Following the eighteenth century, and still prevalent even today, the concept that one region or tract of land could possess unique beneficial features, or that another could be harmful and detrimental to health, has been dismissed as irrelevant and superstitious nonsense. When it is assumed that one site or location is as harmless and suitable for human habitation as any other, it ignores the knowledge that, at a subconscious level, our body, mind and psychic super sensitivities remain highly attuned and are expressed through the supreme intelligence of the cells in our body.

Works cited

Lyall Watson. *Beyond Supernature*, Hodder & Stoughton, London, 1986.

Guy Underwood. *The Pattern of the Past*, Museum Press, London, 1968.

Tom Williamson. *Dowsing: New Light on an Ancient Art*, Robert Hale, London, 1993.

Georges Lakhovsky. *The Secret of Life*, Trans I Reiper, Society of Metaphysicians, 1997.

Michael Shallis. *The Electric Shock Book*, Souvenir Press, London, 1988.

Dr Ernst Hartmann. *Illness as a Problem of Location*, Karl F. Haug Verlag, Heidelberg, 1964.

Herbert L. König. *The Invisible Environment: The Human Being Influenced by Electromagnetic Interactions,* König, Munich, 1975.

Gustav Freiherr von Pohl. *Earth Currents, Causative Factor of Cancer and Other Diseases*, Frech-Verlag, Stuttgart, 1932.

Suggested further reading

L. E. Zaffanella. 'Survey of residential magnetic field sources.' EPRI TR-102759-V1, Project 3335-02. Electric Power Research Institute, Palo Alto, CA, 1993.

Dr A Dubrov. *The Geomagnetic Field and Life,* Plenum Press, New York, 1998.

Käthe Bachler. *Earth Radiation*, Wordmasters, Manchester, 1989.

Thomas Saunders. *The Boiled Frog Syndrome*, (text extracts pp 47–84).

Contact: The British Society of Dowsers is one of the worldwide dowsing organisations (info@britishdowsers.org). It runs teaching courses, conferences and sells dowsing equipment.

APPENDICES

Appendix 1

Negative ions depletion

In a poorly ventilated, dry, airless environment, the lack of negative ions produces a biological reaction in the body that may affect libido, muscles, adrenals, eyes, heart, kidneys, white blood cells and the reproductive system. Negative ion depletion affects our immune systems and may also cause feelings of fatigue. Ions are electrically charged molecules of air gases. They are positive in the ionosphere and negative at the Earth's surface. Negative ions induce a sense of calmness, alertness, quick recovery from illness and a general sense of well-being. When a thunderstorm is brewing, we can feel depressed until the lightning flashes and the thunder cracks; suddenly, the air is fresher and we feel energised and revitalised. The more abundant positive ions continually 'gobble up' negative ions to achieve a balanced state. Once all the available negative ions have been depleted in the air, the positive ions will then deplete the negative ions in the bloodstream and the calcium ions binding brain tissue will be impaired.

Appendix 2

Earthquake-resistant design

The structural earthquake-resistant design of a 37-storey office building in Tokyo for Mitsubishi Corporation has been based on technology devised around a thousand years ago. When the port city of Kobe was shattered by an earthquake in 1995, more than 6,000 people died and swathes of the city were devastated. However, the ancient pagoda remained standing in the midst of the ruins. Nara, Japan's first capital city, has many historical monuments, including a five-storey pagoda built in the eighth century. It too withstood a massive earthquake in the fifteenth century and thousands of other quakes since. There are some five hundred ancient pagodas in Japan and only two have collapsed due to earthquakes.

The pagoda is a wooden tower built as a shrine to house Buddhist relics, and only the priests are allowed to enter the inner sanctum areas. Most are five storeys high although others are considerably taller. None of the storeys are rigidly fixed to each other. The large overhanging eaves are heavily weighted down with roof tiles that act like a balancing pole used by a tightrope walker. Inside, a central column of solid timber runs from top to bottom, and is not attached to the floors. When the floors start to shake from side to side in an earthquake, the timber column acts as a buffer to absorb the violent vibration. The new Mitsubishi office building has been designed with a non-structural central column of 'soft' steel independent of the main structure of the building, which will cushion earthquake vibrations at each floor level. This has yet to be tested in an actual earthquake, but simulators indicate that the building will not collapse.

Appendix 3

The nightingale floor in Nijo Castle, Kyoto

The seventeenth-century palaces and temples in Kyoto are built of timber with translucent screens separating the inner apartments and state rooms from the wide corridor around the perimeter of the building. The corridor flooring is made of wide planks of timber set on joists with each plank fixed by nails hooked on to other nails in the joists underneath the boarding. The nails were 'tuned' so that when a person walks across the floor the slight spring in the boarding causes the nails to rub together and make the dulcet, soothing sound of a nightingale singing. Those asleep in the apartments will be gently but positively alerted by anyone crossing the floor.

Appendix 4

Harmonic ratios

Traditional Japanese architecture is consistent with the teachings of Vitruvius. Room sizes are determined by the size of the tatami woven rush mat. Each mat measures just under 1 metre x 2 metres (3 feet x 6 feet), which is the harmonic proportion 1:2. As every room size is designed according to the module of a tatami, all interior spaces from the smallest to the largest are based on the harmonic proportions of 1:2 or 2:3 or 3:4 and so on, rising along the musical scales and ratios. However diverse the interior spaces and façades may be, the architecture expresses a harmonious, unified whole.